Originally Published as:
Louise Shelly - PNG Cookbook

Port Moresby Community Development Group 1976

Dr. Bruce Yeates, then at UPNG, as one of the original
members of the Port Moresby Community Development
Group suggested and authorised the reprint of this
material.

ISBN:
9980-939-25-7

Cover Design
Peter Leo Ella

Typesetting and Layout:
Philemon Yalamu, *www.artech.com.pg*

Published by:
UniBOOKS (An Original Publication)

UniBOOKS
P.O.Box 413, University PO,
National Capital District,
Papua New Guinea
Phone: 675 + 3267284
Fax: 675 + 3267368

COOK BOOK

Louise Shelly

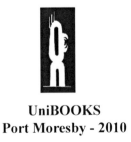

UniBOOKS
Port Moresby - 2010

PNG COOKBOOK

CONTENTS	PAGE

Part 1 – General Information

COOKING IN PAPUA NEW GUINEA

Nothing is more delicious than Highlands kaukau hot from the fire unless it's a mud clam from a mangrove swamp in Milne Bay cooked with fern leaves and coconut cream or Dia, a Central District delicacy combining sago, bananas and thick coconut cream or… It really depends where you are. All villagers are expert in cooking food specific to their area.

Ingredients and cooking methods vary from area to area in Papua New Guinea. As coconuts are common in coastal areas, coconut milk is an essential ingredient in most coastal cooking but in the Highlands the use of the coconut is rare.

In almost all areas food is considered to be divided into three main types edible greens (kumu); meat, fish or poultry (abus); and staples. In some areas cooks will only combine two of these food groups where in others everything can be placed into the same cooking pot. All food groups can be combined in mumu pits. Other than kumu and the staple vegetables, only a few vegetables are used regularly.

Ripe fruit and nuts are usually considered as snack foods so it isn't very common to consider these in meal planning.

The three basic food groups are expanding with the introduction of food from other areas and cultural groups influencing Papua New Guinea. Rice is now a staple all over the country as bread is in the larger centres. Tinned fish and bully beef are eaten in many homes everyday. Chinese cabbage, as well as Western-type cabbage, is popular. Choko leaves are popular in many areas but it was Europeans who introduced the fruit as an edible vegetable.

Probably the strongest influence on ingredients used in Papua New Guinean cooking has been the introduction of foods and spices that increase flavor. Traditionally, coconut, salt and in some areas lemon leaves were about all that were used specifically to enhance the taste of cooked foods.

Coastal women used sea-water for salt and salt in the Highlands was obtained infrequently through trade or from the ashes of fires built on certain rocks near lakes. Ginger, which in many areas is chewed on as a tasty snack, or perhaps for medicinal or magical reasons is now used in some areas to flavour fish dishes. Tomatoes, chilies, onions, and garlic are increasing in popularity and curry powder and pepper are sold n most trade stores.

Traditionally, villagers cook over an open fire. Food is either wrapped in leaves or placed directly into the fire. In some areas the food is cooked in clay pots or green bamboo placed in the fire.

Usually a mumu pit is used to cook for large groups or special events. Some people prefer mumu as an everyday method of cooking. To mumu a large pit is dug, rocks placed in it and a fire lit. When the fire is out and the rocks are red hot a layer of leaves is placed over the rocks so that the food can be placed in the pit. On the coast coconut milk is poured over all the food. Layers of leaves are used to enclose all the food. Then earth or more leaves will be piled on top so that the food can be left to steam for several hours.

By now modern technology has altered many traditional village cooking methods. Almost all villagers have large metal cooking pots to place in the open fire and in many villages kerosene stoves are used to supplement or even replace open fires. Sometimes five gallon drums are used for a smaller menu type meal. Drum ovens are being introduced to many villages so that bread and scone making are becoming popular in some areas.

Many women in towns and cities live in houses equipped with gas or electric stoves. They have adapted many traditional cooking methods to grill ovens besides learning many new techniques.

Most Papua New Guineans eat a large meal in the evening, a small breakfast and no mid-day meal although many town-dwellers are rapidly adapting to take-out sandwiches and pies at noon.

A woman in Papua New Guinea always cooks a lot of food in the evenings will have enough food for any wantoks who come by around mealtime besides leftovers for her family's morning meal. Both the cooking and growing this food is important to her. She is proud that she doesn't waste any. Scraps can be used to grow new food or to feed the animals.

Currently there is no cookbook published that is exclusively Papua New Guinean. Occasionally groups around the country have put out collections but often these have had more European recipes and ingredients in them than local.

A number of groups and individuals here are actively promoting the collection of distinctively local recipes but recipe collecting is difficult. A village woman here does not think in terms of exact methods and measure-ments that would be easy to write down. She learned to cook by working with older women in the village and now young girls are learning by helping Women in towns share methods from their home villages by talking and cooking together. Only a very few women with Western educations may share cooking ideas by writing recipes down for each other.

Part 1: General Information

2

A lot of the cooking doesn't need exactly this or that - a woman merely uses what she has. If there's lots of coconuts available that day she'll make a richer soup. If there's no taro or kaukau then she'll cook up tapioca with whatever else is around.

Often when you ask a Papua New Guinean woman for a recipe she'll give you a description which will only be meaningful if you have had some previous understanding of the basic cooking methods. It's probably best to learn more about Papua New Guinean cooking by following the custom here. Cook with your friends. People are only too eager to teach you once you show an initial interest in both the eating and the cooking.

To get you started cooking with Papua New Guinean foods this recipe collection has a section to describe the most common vegetables, greens and fruits with notes on how to use them. The small selection of PNG recipes is to start you collecting more of your own.

The larger selection of recipes included here are from Asia, Australia and the South Pacific besides a few adapted Canadian ones. They only use foods grown locally apart from spices and dairy products.

ABUS

Fish, turtle, live chickens, and some bush animals are available in the markets. Other meat is raised in the villages or bought from butchers.

Beef is relatively cheap but chicken and pork are quite expensive and definitely luxury foods. The cheapest way to buy this type of meat is whole and learn to do your own butchering.

Chicken would be the easiest to start with. Choose plump birds with soft smooth legs and tender skin. The end of the breastbone should be flexible and soft and the eyes should be bright. An old bird has hard, dry scaly legs, a hard breastbone and long hairs.

Learn what times fresh fish arrives at your market (if it does) and be there then as markets here don't have proper storing facilities. Also good fish is rapidly sold out.

When buying brightly coloured fish, check whether they have poison sacks and learn how to remove them when necessary.

A fresh fish has firm flesh, bright eyes, and red gills. Poke the eyes and lift up the gills to ensure your fish is fresh.

3

Fish which is sold smoked keeps much longer in the market. Often this fish must be soaked before eating.

When buying shellfish make sure they are tightly closed. If the shells are beginning to open, the animal is dying and the meat beginning to decay. Leave in fresh water for several minutes before cooking to remove sand and mud from the shell-fish. Boil in shells. When cooked, the shells will open and you can remove the meat.

Turtle meat must also be very fresh. Usually they are killed one at a time and cut up right at the market for immediate sale. Boil in coconut cream.

How to fillet a fish: Wash the fish thoroughly in cold water and pat dry with paper towels. Take a sharp knife and holding fish firmly by tail (use a cloth to prevent slipping), remove the scales by scraping down towards the head. Next sever the head at the gills, remove all fins and finally the tail. Make a long straight opening right down the fish belly and remove the guts. Wash fish again and open to remove backbone. You should now be able to cut the fish down the back, thus making two whole fillets. However, if it is a small fish with small bones, this may mutilate the fish too much, so leave the backbone in. Flatfish are not boned. Some may prefer to cook the fish whole, but it still should be scaled and the gut removed by slitting the belly open enough to remove same. Now you have the fish ready to cook in a number of ways.

Cooking Fresh Crab and Lobster: You must drown them first in FRESH water in a bucket. Then place in a large saucepan, cover with cold water and bring to the boil, simmer until cooked (lobster will turn bright red). Do not overcook as this will toughen the flesh. Break off a claw to test doneness. It usually takes about 20, minutes. Serve hot with sauce, if liked, or cold with salad. Crab is usually eaten cold. Lobster is very good with curry or cheese sauce. Remove "coral" from the lobster and serve separately to those who like it. Both can be served very decoratively, but this is not necessary.

KUMU

E **dible Greens:** The markets all over PNG are filled with a wide variety of green leaves which are both delicious and highly nutritious once you learn how to cook with them. Besides they are much more economical than the slightly nutritious lettuce that is imported from Australia at fantastic prices.

It's difficult to learn names for all the kumu available as they may

kumu..

4

only have local names or of course botanical names. If you ask a woman in the market what the name of a particular leaf is she'll look at you in a puzzled way or perhaps reply, "kumu tasol". Don't try to learn the greens by name; learn to recognize them by shape, color and taste. You'll soon have your favorites.

When you buy a new kumu cook a little bit and taste it before adding it to your food or serving it for a meal. Some are bitter when cooked, others will change consistency when cooked, some will not blend well with other kumu and others will not suit the other food you are cooking. As most of this is a matter of taste you will have to do your own experimenting to discover which ones you'll use again. Take time to discover the various greens available in your market, as they're probably some of the most exciting local vegetables available.

Many kumu are sold with roots or stalks that can be replanted in your garden. So it's also important to learn which parts of your vegetables can be used to grow more.

Only buy your greens on the day you intend to cook with them and as close to cooking time as possible. If you have to store them for a few hours, soak them in water or wet them and wrap in a tea towel to be placed in the fridge. If you have a garden you can pick your vegetables just before throwing them in the pot.

You must be careful not to overcook your greens as they will lose a lot of food value and become mushy and unappetizing. Always add greens to a soup to-wards the end of cooking. This isn't possible when mumuing but it doesn't seem to matter as when boiling or frying. Also learn to fry greens Chinese-style which is by far the best method to retain food value and taste.

Aibika Leaves: Aibika, tapioca and pawpaw leaves all have a general maple leaf shape. Only aibika are eaten in PNG. Sometimes Aibika leaves may have a slight red tinge on them especially on the stalks. As aibika is a very popular green it's almost always available in the markets.

Use only the young top leaves which are fresh and green. Prepare by removing the tough stalk and the old tough leaves.

..kumu

Aibika leaves are used in coconut soups and as part of mumued dishes as well as for edible wrappings for many dishes.

If you are adding aibika leaves to a coconut cream soup it is a good idea to partly boil them to remove the gluey substance that can come out of them.

To use these leaves as part of a European-type meal cook the whole leave in boiling water for 2 minutes, turn and cook for another 2 minutes.   Serve with coconut cream or butter. Do not overcook or they will become slimy.

SEASONINGS: basil, oregano, rosemary, tarragon

Chinese Cabbage: (*Brassica chinesis*) Use the green tender leaves and firm white stalks. Prepare by removing the tough lower parts of the stalks and tough outer leaves. Wash well.

Use whole or chop into diagonal strips. Chinese cabbage can be boiled in salted water or coconut cream, used in soups or stews, sautéed lightly or served raw in salads.

To serve as part of a Western-type meal, remove leaf from stalk and cut the leaves and stalks into diagonal strips. Boil stalks 3 to 4 minutes in salted water. Add leaves and boil for a further 2 to 3 minutes. Drain and season with butter.

Another method: Sauté washed leaves in a little butter or oil in a pan. Add a little water, cover and steam until tender. Season with salt.

Or: Sauté a little onion and garlic in oil or butter. Add prepared cabbage and sauté 2 to 3 minutes. Add a little water and cook until tender.

SEASONINGS: basil, oregano, rosemary, tarragon

Ota Fern (*Athyrium esculenta*) Use the young fresh green leaves only. To prepare remove the leafy parts by running your thumb and forefinger along the tough stem and ribs. Don't press too hard or you will bruise the leaves.

Ferns must be cooked very quickly and lightly to preserve their flavour and food value. Always add them last to any dish you are boiling or frying. Dishes made from coconut cream enhance the flavour of ota fern.

Fry in a little oil or butter for a minute and then squeeze thick coconut cream into the pan and continue cooking for another minute or two.

If serving with a western type meal, boil in salted water for two to minutes. Drain and serve with butter and a slice of lemon or with Miti sauce. (included in this collection, page 99)

SEASONINGS: basil, garlic, marjoram, mustard, savory, thyme
Pumpkin Tips and Sweet Potato Tops: Use the young shoots with crisp stems and young leaves. To prepare remove the tough leaves and thick lower part of the stems. It is easy to snap the crisp top

kumu..

6

part of the stem away from the tougher, stringier lower section. Many cooks prefer to remove the strings from the pumpkin tips.

Can be boiled in coconut cream or added to mumus.

To serve as a European style vegetable, cook in boiling salted water for 2 to 5 minutes and serve with butter.

SEASONINGS: basil, dill, parsley, tarragon

Taro Leaves: (*Colocasia esculenta*)
(Dalo Leaves)

Choose young leaves with green stems. Old leaves and those from certain purple stemmed varieties, contain oxalate crystals which can irritate the mouth and throat. It's best to cook taro leaves for ten minutes on each side to avoid itchiness.

Finely chopped, young taro leaves can give a lift to food in the same way as chopped garlic is used in cooking.

To prepare wash well and remove the tough lower stem; scrape on the outside and soak in water with cover for 30 minutes.

Taro leaves can be boiled in coconut cream or used as edible food wrappings when steaming, baking or boiling.

As part of a western type meal, boil in salted water or bake in the oven and serve with butter or thick coconut cream.

SEASONING: basil, dill, parsley, tarragon

Tulip: (*Gnetum gnemon*)
Paired edible leaves which grow on a tree known by the same name in Pidgin.

Some of these are sweet but others are bitter and it is very hard to tell merely by looking. It's best to cook one or two in a little water for tasting before adding to the rest of your food. Can be used in coconut cream dishes or mumus.

..kumu

Watercress: (*Nasturtium officinale*)
Use the young stems with large leaves. Remember to wash well in several changes of water as it tends to harbour parasites.

Watercress can be boiled in salted water or coconut cream or served raw in salads or with mit (page 99).

It can also be cooked in chicken stock and used as a base for cream soup.

SEASONINGS: basil, dill, parsley, tarragon

Water Spinach (*Basella alba*)
(Indian Spinach)

Use young stems with large tender leaves. Water spinach should be washed very well and stored in plastic bags or covered containers if not used immediately.

Use as other greens in traditional food and always add towards the last 5-10 minutes. Don't overcook as it will become sticky.

Cook leaves in a small quantity of boiling salted water for 3 to 4 minutes. Drain, season with butter or coconut cream.

Cook in a saucepan with a little butter, stirring frequently until soft.

SEASONINGS: basil, dill, nutmeg, tarragon.

Inedible Greens: Oversize leaves such as banana leaves, tankard leaves, breadfruit leaves, betel nut leaves, canna leaves, or tapioca leaves can be used as wrappings for food to be baked, steamed or mumued.

Wash well before using and remove before serving the food. To soften leaves for wrapping, hold for a minute over a flame or dip in boiling water.

It is possible to substitute tin-foil in recipes that call for any of these leaves as wrappings but the taste won't be quite the same. It is also possible to use brown paper or cloth.

These leaves are also used to wrap food to keep it fresh and clean.

Papaya leaves contain high amounts of papain which is the base of all meat tenderizers. So wrap your tough steaks in papaya leaves and let stand for several hours. Papaya juice is used in the same way.

STAPLES staples

*T*here is a wide variety of starchy foods which are eaten as staples in Papua New Guinea as well as the rest of the South Pacific. Only the sweet potato (kaukau) is similar to foods eaten by most Canadians. Probably you will like most of these foods immediately but a few like sago may take a little time. After a while many people living here begin to think of the 'English potato' as a poor second best to the variety of alternatives available in the markets here.

Breadfruit: (*Artocarpus altilis*) Although used as a staple, breadfruit is technically a fruit and not a vegetable. Choose fruit which is fully formed and firm and a pale yellow green in colour. Ripe fruit is soft and has a sweet flavour. Care must be taken to keep it quite cool to prevent the fruit from becoming over-ripe. Half ripe fruit will keep for 1 or 2 days.

Store breadfruit in a bucket of water or refrigerator.

Traditionally the peeled and wedged fruit is boiled in coconut milk or added to mumus. The whole fruit is roasted unpeeled over an open fire or charcoal.

Sometimes the sap from the fruit is used as glue.

To prepare wedges for cooking, peel stem, cut in halves or quarters, and serve with butter, salt and pepper.

To bake; wash, puncture with a skewer and bake at 350 for 1 to 12 hours or until soft. Test with a skewer. Cut in wedges and serve with butter.

Alternatively wash and remove core and stem; place 2 T butter and 2 T in the cavity; replace stem and bake until tender.

Cook whole fruit over hot coals, turning frequently. Slice and fry.

Bake with a roast.

Use cooked breadfruit for chips.

SEASONINGS: bay leaf, caraway, celery seed/salt, coriander, dill, fennel seed, garlic, mace, marjoram, mustard, paprika, parsley, poppy seed

Cooking Bananas: (*Musa spp.*)
(Plantains, vudi)

staples

Many varieties of bananas are only digestible when cooked fully ripe. (Some wild bananas in PNG are completely inedible or cooked.) All green bananas as well as cooking bananas contain mostly starch and so can be cooked as a supplement to other staples but must not be eaten to the exclusion, of other more nutritious staples such as kaukau, taro and yam. When eating bananas ripe they turn to sugar and so are only used for sweets if cooked. Sweet bananas tend to make dishes sappy and so should not be used in place of green or cooking bananas.

To store bananas, hang the bunch in a cool place.

Green bananas are difficult to peel and also stain the hands. There are two ways to peel a green banana.

(1) Rub the hands with oil and oil the knife, then peel like a potato.
(2) Place green bananas in boiling water for 5-10 minutes. The peel will then lift off quite easily.

Traditionally cooking bananas are boiled in coconut milk, added to mumus, or smoke in their peel in the ashes of an open fire.

Boil or steam long green eating bananas with their skins on until tender. Boil whole cooking bananas without their skins until tender. Skin, slice length-wise and fry slowly until crisp. Season with salt or sugar if desired. Pepper and crushed chilies are good too. Ripe bananas are best for this.

Boil, mash, add cinnamon, sugar and milk or coconut milk.

Skin, slice thinly in circles and fry with salt in fat.

Makes an excellent thickening for meat, soup and stews when grated and added in.

Slice thinly and fry for chips.

Half cook, peel and roast in hot fat or oil and serve with meat.

SEASONINGS: bay leaf, caraway, celery seed/salt, coriander, dill, fennel seed, garlic, mace, marjoram, mustard, paprika, parsley, poppy seed

Part 1: General Information

staples

Kaukau: (*Ipomea batatas*)
(Sweet potato, kumala, kumara)

Many of the varieties of kaukau grown in PNG are similar in appearance and taste to the sweet potatoes available in Canada, but others are long and tubular-shaped and others are quite large with less definite shapes. Kaukau flesh ranges in color from purple to yellow to white to white with purplish spots. To the unfamiliar eye it is not always possible to determine the inside colour by the outward appearance of the kaukau. White fleshed and purple fleshed kaukau is not as sweet nor as nutritious as the yellow varieties.

Choose roots that are sound and free from holes as the sweet potato is frequently attacked by a borer insect. Although more perishable than English potatoes, kaukau will keep for 3-4 weeks or more if stored on open wire shelves or a similar well ventilated place.

As kaukau is a favorite staple with both Papua New Guineans and Europeans here, there is a long list of cooking suggestions.

They are delicious baked in an open fire or as part of a mumu or boiled in coconut cream.

To retain their full nutriment, kaukau must be cooked with their jackets on.

Scrub well and steam or boil in the skin. Peel when cooked and serve with melted butter and chopped parsley.

Peel, parboil and place in hot fat or oil and roast. Excellent served with pork.

Cook and mash with butter, salt and pepper and scallop.

Cook and mash with thick coconut cream.

Bake the kaukau in its skin, scoop out flesh and mash with a little butter and port wine. Season with salt and pepper. Refill shells and brown in oven.

staples

Use in soups, stews or curries.

Use as potatoes in potato salads.

Peel and bake dry on oven shelf. Remove the top of the potato and scoop insides. Mix with chopped onion and chopped bacon. Replace mixture in potato, putting lid back on. Bake until completely cooked - that is, when skin can be easily pierced - about 20 minutes in a moderate oven. Once again remove lid, and cover with grated cheese. Place under griller until cheese melts.

Boil kaukau until almost soft. Make a candy of 1 cup brown sugar and 2 oz. of butter. Melt ingredients (do not boil), until mixture turns to thick, candy-like substance. Place kaukau in a casserole, pour syrup over gently and heat until required.

SEASONINGS: allspice, cinnamon, clove, ginger, mace, nutmeg, poppy seed

Sago: (*Metroxylon sagu, Metroxylon rumphii*) Sago is made by beating the root of the sago palm into a powder. This powder is a light beige colour and can have purplish or greenish streaks in it. It is best when fresh and soft. Sago will harden but doesn't go bad. It is possible to re-wash hard sago to soften it and then to redry it in the sun.

In the markets sago is sold in plastic bags or bundles, wrapped in banana leaves and tied with dried grass. Check with the vendors as the appearance of these bundles varies from area to area. Often it is a rectangular shape.

Keep sago sealed to preserve its freshness longer. Plastic bags are good.

Sago sometimes is used as a thickner, similarly to cornstarch, but mostly it is eaten as a staple food in PNG.

You probably will need to develop a taste for sago.

Fry lightly in an ungreased pan until it is crumbly. Then mix with freshly grated coconut.

Mince with grated coconut and enough water from the coconut to form the mixture into small cakes and bake.

Use in pancakes and puddings.

staples

Tapioca Roots: (*Manihot esculenta*)
(Cassava, manioc, yuca)
Tapioca is grown in most village gardens to be used at times when sweet potatoes, taro or yams are unavailable as it is not quite as nutritious as these other foods. In areas where there are seasonal droughts, tapioca is a regular feature of the diet.

This plant, which is a member of the poinsettia family, can grow to 10 feet in rich soil, producing long-stalked, hand-shaped leaves. It has a long, irregularly-shaped starchy root at least 2 inches in diameter with a rough brown bark-like skin and hard white interior.

Freshly dug tapioca will last 2-3 days when stored in a cool place or to 2 or 3 weeks if refrigerated.

Before preparing tapioca, break a root to see that it is white inside and does not contain hard fibres. Blue streaks in the flesh indicate that the roots are not fresh. Never eat raw tapioca, as the raw root contains hydrocyanic acid in its juices, which is poisonous. The toxic properties are destroyed by heat or removed by repeated washings. [Editor's note: This is because tapioca varieties in Papua New are almost all "sweet". "Bitter" varieties should also be processed by scraping the roots.]

Tapioca roots are skinned rather than peeled. Take the tip of a knife and rip the skin off similarly to the method you would use to peel an orange. Slice in 2 to 4 inch lengths to ensure thorough cooking. Some cooks prefer to break the tapioca into small pieces and then split lengthwise. This way the stringy fibres in the centre can be removed.

Tapioca can be boiled, baked, steamed or fried to serve as a staple vegetable. Many Westerners tend to like it better when cooked in thick coconut cream or as thick chips.

It can be eaten in pieces or mashed and combined with meat, fish or onion and seasonings.

Boil well and when cooked (but firm) put through a mincer or chop finely; then add pepper and salt. Make into small cakes and fry until brown in dripping or butter.

Grated tapioca takes on glutinous properties when cooked. Use this in for tapioca balls or to thicken stews and sauces and puddings.

In Asia and some parts of the South Pacific, the starch is extracted and dried to be used instead of cornflour.

SEASONINGS: bay leaf, caraway, celery seed/salt, coriander, dill, fennel seed, garlic, mace, marjoram, mustard, paprika, parsley, poppy seed.

Taro: (*Colocasia esculenta*) (Dalo, Talo)
There are numerous varieties of taro roots. Some have a white or yellow dry texture when cooked, others have a flesh of a blue-grey, or purple to red color and a cheese-like texture.

13

The roots should be freshly dug and must be firm to the touch. If kept in a cool dry place, the roots stay in good condition for 3-4 days and much longer if refrigerated.

Care must be taken when peeling certain purple stemmed varieties of taro as the peel can contain oxalate crystals which irritate the skin when moistened and also the mouth and throat. Make sure your hands are perfectly dry before peeling taro and don't rub any parts of your body while peeling. It's wisest to hold the taro by its thick stem, place it on a level surface and peel downwards. Women well experienced in peeling taro never actually touch the peel or flesh. It is also important to remove any rings of peel that may be embedded in the flesh of the root or your mouth may itch when eating.

Taro is popular in mumus where it is baked whole. In many areas it is considered an essential ingredient along with yams.

Taro can be broken or chopped into pieces to be boiled in coconut cream.

Alternatively you could wrap the taro in tankard leaves or aluminum foil before baking in an open fire or an oven.

For western type meals, peel the taro and cut in halves; bake in the oven, and serve with butter, salt and pepper.

Cut the taro in slices; soak in several changes of water to remove the starch and steam or boil.

Make taro into chips.

Use taro in soups and stews and curries instead of potatoes.

Use taro instead of potatoes in potato salads.

Cooked tender taro is good when sliced a ½ inch thick and browned quickly in a little oil or butter and seasoned to taste.

Peel, wash and cut into pieces. Boil for 3 minutes and then grate the taro finely. Squeeze lemon, onion, and chili juice on top.

staples

Boil in a little salted water, strain and cool. When cold, cut into ¼ to 1 inch wedges and dry in melted butter until browned on both sides. Serve buttered slices; especially nice with syrup, jam or melted cheese.

Part 1: General Information

14

For a barbecue, roll taro in banana or tankard leaves and bake in the ashes.

SEASONINGS: bay leaf, caraway, celery seed/salt, coriander, dill, fennel seed, garlic, mace, marjoram, mustard, paprika, parsley, poppy seed

TOK PISIN: taro, taro kanaka

Chinese Taro: (*Xanthosoma sagittifolium*) Small sized potato type roots with a fairly rough outer skin and red or white flesh.

Choose tubers which are firm and free from blemishes. If stored on wire racks, Chinese taro will keep for 2 to 3 weeks. No precautions need to be taken when peeling Chinese taro as with taro itself.

Use in the same way as taro.

Yams (*Dioscorea esculenta*)
(Tivoli, kawai, ufi, mami)
These are large tuberous vegetables that may weigh as much as 100 pounds. The skin is thick and somewhat hairy and the flesh may be white, yellow, red or purple. It is quite starchy and has a subtle flavour; somewhat nutlike.

In some areas yams are an integral part of traditional ceremonies. Yam houses are built on some of the islands to display the villagers wealth of yams.

Do not confuse the tropical yam with the North American term yam which is often applied to the soft orange-coloured sweet potato.

Choose firm, clean roots that will keep for several months stored on open wire shelves or other well ventilated areas.

To prepare yams; scrub, cut off the hairs and peel if you prefer.

The yam is popular roasted in an open fire or mumu or boiled in coconut cream.

staples

Yams can also be used in a wide variety of ways for Western-style meals.

Punch holes in the skin with a skewer; bake and serve with butter.

Peel, and steam or boil. Then mash or fry whole or in pieces or slices.

Use yams as potatoes as described under kaukau and taro.

Use in soups, stews and curries.

Cut yam into ½ inch slices, soaking these in several lots of water until the final one is starch free (about 4 hours). Then dry the pieces and roll in seasoned flour and deep fry.

Scrub yams and bake in their skin. Cut off the top, scoop out the flesh and mash with salt, pepper and butter. Add a little milk or coconut cream. (Also grated cheese, coconut or onion). Refill and brown in the oven.

Boil in a little salted water, strain and cool. When cold, cut into ¼ to ½ wedges and fry in melted butter until browned on both sides. Serve slices, especially nice with syrup, jam or melted cheese.

Boil in salted water, drain well and reheat. Mash and add milk powder to dry it, a dot of butter and the chopped green tops of shallots.

Grate raw yam, season well and drop by spoonfuls in boiling fat and fry until well-cooked.

Grate two cupfuls of raw yam, add ½ cup cornflour, salt and pepper to taste. Beat well and drop by spoonfuls into boiling fat. They rise into balls. Lie on well browned, drain on paper and serve hot.

SEASONINGS: allspice, cinnamon, clove, ginger, mace, nutmeg, poppy seed

TOK PISIN: mami; yam

COCONUTS

Wherever coconuts grow they serve multiple purposes within the life and economy of many coastal villages. This section will just describe some of the uses for coconuts within the kitchen.

Young Coconuts: Young coconuts have a light green skin and a light-colored husk. These coconuts are prized for drinking. The fresher the young coconut, the sweeter the water.

coconuts

When the coconut is young it is fairly easy to remove the top with a bush knife or large cleaver.

The meat is only beginning to form in young coconuts and is easily peeled away from the shell with your fingers once the liquid has

16

been drunk. It is very delicious to eat as is.

You may also want to eat the young coconut flesh with fresh fruit such as pawpaw, bananas or mangoes. It is also good as a topping for sweet desserts.

Mature Coconuts: Mature coconuts have thick, firm meat and plenty of liquid. The husk is dark brown with a yellowish skin. To break the husk away from the nut, use a sharp-ended tool. Use the husks for scouring pots, scrubbing floors or straining coconut cream.

When selecting a mature coconut, shake or tap it to see that it still contains plenty of water. If the coconut is very full you may not hear the liquid but tapping the shell will produce a dull thud. Dry old coconuts will sound definitely hollow.

Check to see that the "eyes" are not moldy or wet as this may mean the coconut is spoiled.

Some people will tell you never to buy a coconut if one of the eyes is beginning to sprout at all. Other people will tell you the coconut, is better tasting when it is beginning to sprout a little. Try both kinds and decide which you prefer.

Mature coconuts with sprouting eyes may have a white growth inside them. This pulp is quite edible just as it is. Some people consider it a treat.

To drain the water from a mature coconut, you must puncture two of the three dark eyes. Hammer the eyes with the sharp tip of an ice pick or drive a screwdriver through them.

Coconut water can be safely kept in the refrigerator for 2 or 3 ays or in the freezer for several weeks.

The liquid inside a coconut should always be referred to as coconut water, not coconut milk. Coconut milk or cream is made by squeezing grated coconut.

An easier way to break a coconut in two halves is to hold and toss it in one hand while hammering an imaginary line around the middle with a hammer, the blunt end of a meat-cleaver or the edge of a bush knife. It's worthwhile to have this demonstrated to you. People who can break coconuts this way can quickly catch the liquid in a bowl just as the nut breaks in two.

coconuts

You can lie the coconut on a solid surface such as concrete and give it a sharp tap or two at the middle with a heavy knife. Then you should be able to pull the two halves apart. If you want to loosen

Part 1: General Information

the meat inside the shell, drain the liquid, then hold the coconut in one hand and tap around the outside in a dozen or more different places (not in a line as when breaking the nut in halves.) Use the blunt edge of a cleaver or bush knife, a kitchen mallet or even a hammer. When the shell begins to split, give the coconut one or two sharp blows with the implement to break it.

The meat should fall away from the shell in large sections. If not, rap the out-side of each piece to loosen the meat further and then cut it out with a small knife.

Alternately you could drain the liquid from the coconut and then place it in a shallow pan and place the pan in a 300 F oven for 45 minutes. If the nut doesn't crack on its own tap it lightly with a hammer. It should then be fairly easy to remove the meat from the shell.

If you already have your coconut in halves and want to remove the meat in pieces, take a sharp, sturdy knife and cut deeply into the flesh to make several cross patterns. Scoop the flesh out of the shell with a strong, broad-bladed knife or something similar.

Once you have removed the meat, you will have a strong coconut shell which can be used for fuel, soup-bowls, pots for plants or to carve into ornaments.

Coconut Cream: Coconut cream or milk is made by squeezing grated coconut to remove all the moisture from the meat.

You will need a coconut scraper to grate the coconut. If you use a coconut scraper, you must divide the coconut in half but not remove the meat. It is removed by scraping.

Coconut scrapers in PNG are usually small stools with one elongated end fitted with a metal tooth that has a jagged edge. More portable scrapers are boards with one elongated end holding a steel scraper. To scrape the coconut, you must straddle the stool or board (place on a chair) and briskly scrape each half of your coconut over the jagged tooth many times until you have grated all the meat inside the nut. Use a light hand as the finer the scrapings, the richer your coconut cream will be.

coconuts

Alternatively you could remove the flesh from the shell and grate it on a coarse household grater or use an Osterizer if you have one. Once you have grated the coconut you will then squeeze the liquid out of it to make coconut cream.

To do this, add tap water to the scrapings or the liquid from the coconut. It seems to help to add some hot water to the scrapings and let them stand for a little while before squeezing. The amount of water you add will depend on how rich you want the coconut cream. For a thick, rich cream add 1 T water to 1 cup of grated coconut, for a medium rich cream add ½ cup of water to 1 cup of grated coconut . For soups add 1 cup of water to 1 cup of grated coconut. Often for feast dishes no water is added at all. Up to 30 coconuts may be squeezed to make a very rich cream.

Squeeze the grated coconut and liquid with your hands several times to remove as much of the goodness from the grated flesh as possible. Then squeeze it all through a strainer into a bowl or the cooking pot. In some villages the women squeeze the cream through coconut husk to remove the scrapings.

It is easy to strain the cream through cheese-cloth or a clean tea-towel. Using this method it is possible to wring the cloth and remove the liquid even more thoroughly.

Water can be added to the scrapings a 2nd time to make a watery coconut milk suitable for boiling rice in.

Coconut cream contains some protein and when boiled the protein curdles and separates out. In some dishes this doesn't matter but in others the consistency and flavor are spoiled by boiling the cream. Usually recipes will warn you when to avoid boiling. Probably it's best to cook most coconut cream dishes at simmering point. It also helps to cook with the lid off whenever possible. Some recipes require that the lid is on to steam some of the ingredients. Usually it doesn't matter if the cream starts to curdle in these dishes.

If you are having a lot of trouble with curdling coconut cream, try adding a little cornflour soaked in water before bringing the cream to a boil. Remember coconut cream can also curdle when reheating dishes containing coconut milk.

coconuts

To keep coconut milk for a few days, bring it to a boil with a small amount of salt before storing in the refrigerator. Coconut cream can be frozen.

There are countless uses for both grated coconut and coconut cream. The following are a few.

1. Coastal women rinse their hair with grated coconut or coconut cream or oil.

19

2. If you add lemon juice to the grated coconut before squeezing then the left over coconut has more flavor.
3. Add chilies to the grated coconut before squeezing for more flavor.
4. To toast coconut, spread thinly in a shallow pan and brown at 350 F for 8-10 minutes.
5. Rather than scraping coconut for toasting, peel it with a vegetable peeler.
6. Bake grated coconut and sugar for a sweet.
7. Fry grated coconut with brown sugar for a sweet.
8. Add grated coconut to salads.
9. Flavor grated coconut with cinnamon for a topping.
10. Use left-over coconut scrapings for white sauce to serve with creamed vegetables or fish.
11. Scraped coconut is a neutrilizer for chili. If you've rubbed chili on your skin, remedy the burning sensation with a little scraped coconut.
12. Grate 10 coconuts for 3 cups of water. Boil until clear to make coconut oil.
13. Substitute coconut cream for milk in plain scones. These are slightly richer with a delicate coconut flavour which is savoury rather than sweet.
14. Fry green vegetables such as beans and water spinach in hot coconut milk.
15. Simmer thick coconut cream with sugar to make a topping for desserts.
16. Add grated coconut to salads.
17. Put grated coconut in a heavy frying pan with a little sugar and heat to allow the coconut to absorb as much of the sugar as possible. Dry the mixture out but be careful not to burn it. Add cocoa with sugar if desired.

VEGETABLES

Although only green pawpaw, pitpit, pumpkin, beans and taro stalks along with kumu are commonly eaten by Papua New Guineans, many other vegetables are grown especially for the European and Chinese market. Descriptions of those that may not be too familiar to newcomers are included in this section.

Avocado: (*Persea americana*) Avocados are fully developed when they are green, so may be picked green and left to ripen. vegetables

Some are purplish or brown when ripe. Ripe avocados are soft to touch. The peel comes off easily and the seed does not stick to the flesh. A toothpick goes in easily where the stem has come off the fruit. Avocado is only good ripe. Keep ripe avocados in the refrigerator. Ripe fruit may be deep frozen whole in their skin.

Part 1: General Information

20

With a sharp knife, halve avocados length-wise and twist the halves in opposite directions. Strike the seed sharply with a knife, twist and remove.

To slice or cube, hold the avocado cut-side down in the palm of your hand. Begin at the top and peel away the skin. Place it on a cutting board and slice crosswise or lengthwise or chop.

The cut fruit turns black very quickly. To prevent this, sprinkle with lemon or lime juice or vinegar. Wrap in foil or wax paper.

Use raw or just heated through. Do not boil as this develops an unpleasant flavour.

Cut thinly and put on buttered bread with salt and pepper.

Halve, remove the seed and sprinkle with salt and pepper or marinate in French dressing.

Use in salads, or mashed for sandwich fillings.

Use in savory cocktails.

Use in soups and dips.

Use in desserts.

Beans: Several varieties of beans are found in the markets including the French-style beans Canadians are used to. Other varieties found here are: **Long Beans: (Cow Peas)** These beans grow up to 6 or 7 inches long. Papua New Guineans prefer these beans fairly mature although you often can find young green ones in the market.

Use long beans as soon as possible after you buy them but if you need to store them, wash and place in a plastic bag or covered container and keep in the refrigerator or a cool place.

Beans

To prepare, cut diagonally in thin slices with a very sharp knife or razor blade.

Use in Papua New Guinean dishes along with greens.

Simmer in coconut cream for 15 minutes. Add seasonings to taste: chilies, curry powder, onion, garlic, tomatoes.

Cook in boiling, salted water for 5 minutes. Season with a little butter and pepper.

For variation, flavor with a little fresh chopped basil.

Blanch a few okari nuts, cut in fine slices, sauté in butter until golden and toss with beans.

Use cold in salads and in vegetable curries. Use seeds from mature beans in curries.

Boil seeds and serve as a vegetable or substitute for kidney bean in chili or salads.

Winged Beans: (Goa) Choose small young beans and store similarly to long beans.

To prepare trim off ends and part of the frilly edge. Slice diagonally and treat similarly to long beans.

Shell beans into a bowl.

Add lemon or lime juice, salt, pepper, oil and chopped green onions. Allow to marinate before serving.

Sword Beans: Treat similarly to long beans. Remove strings when preparing and cook a little longer than long beans.

SEASONINGS: basil, chili powder, cinnamon, cloves, cumin, curry powder, dill, garlic, mint, mustard, nutmeg, oregano, paprika, parsley, savory, sesame seed, thyme

TOK PISIN: bin

BAMBOO SHOOT

Bamboo Shoots: When peeled the tender shoots of bamboo are very delicious boiled, steamed, stir-fried, or baked.

Boil quickly in salted water or coconut cream and serve with butter.

bamboo

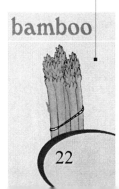

Bake in the oven or fire with skin on. Peel and eat the soft center.

Combine with other vegetables.

Fry with onion and garlic. Flavour with soya Sauce.

TOK PISIN: mambu

Chinese Radish: (*Raphanus sativus*)
(White Radish)

A textured whitish root up to 18 inches or so long. Choose young crisp roots as older roots tend to become very hot. These vegetables will keep for several days on racks. To prepare wash and peel or scrape. Use in soups, stews, curries and Chinese dishes. Grate or slice thinly and use raw in salads. Use in Pickles.

SEASONINGS: caraway, mint, mustard, oregano, parsley, poppy seed, rosemary, sage.

Choko: (*Sechium edule*) (Chocko, Chayote, Cristophene) Choko is somewhat pear-shaped, with rough light green to white skin, and white flesh somewhat firmer than melon flesh.

Choose clean firm fruit. Watch for light brown spots which indicate decay. Also, there should be no sign of the fruit sprouting at the end which indicates an old stringy fruit.

Choko will keep for several days stored on wire racks.

Peel under running water to prevent staining. Cut in halves, quarters or dice. Use in curries or stews.

Boil in salted water until tender and serve with white sauce, cheese or tomato flavoured sauce. Use cold-diced choko in salads. Toss in French dressing and garnish with chives.

Stuff and bake. Boil in water with sugar and cloves as a substitute for tinned pears. Use instead of melons in jams or pickles. Use instead of cucumbers in pickles.

SEASONINGS: cinnamon, dill, garlic, mace, margarine, mustard, nutmeg, paprika, parsley, savory,' tarragon, thyme.

choko

Part 1: General Information

23

EGGPLANT

Eggplant: (*Solanum melongena*)
(Aubergine, Baigan, Baigani)

Although this vegetable is found in Canada, it is not commonly used. Here it is cheap and usually easy to find.

Choose a firm fully developed fruit that is not hard on the ends. Over-ripe eggplant is soft and tends to be full of seeds. Colour is not an indication of ripeness as varieties vary from dark purple to white.

Stored on wire racks or covered in the refrigerator, eggplant keeps for several days.

Peel fruit if desired, slice or cube and soak in salted water for 20 minutes to prevent discoloration.

Slice, place in a pie-dish; add sliced onion, salt, and a chopped chili, cover with thick coconut cream and bake slowly in a moderate oven.

Bake whole in the ashes of an open fire; serve with lemon juice, salt and chilies.

Use in soups, stews, curries, or casseroles.

Use as a base for soup.

Cut in slices, dip in milk or egg and flour or in butter and fry.

Leave skin on, scoop out centre and stuff with meat or vegetables.

SEASONINGS: allspice, anise, bay leaf, chili powder, coriander, garlic, parsley, and sage

Ginger Root: (*Zingiber officinale*) Ginger root is a gnarled, brown root about 3 inches long with a more pungent flavour than dried ground ginger. It is sold in bunches in the markets.

In some areas of PNG ginger root is considered as a tasty snack to chew on and in many areas it is used in sorcery. Nowadays some women are beginning to use crushed or sliced ginger to flavor fish and other dishes.

Whole fresh ginger root will keep for a few weeks wrapped in a plastic bag in the refrigerator.

Part 1: General Information

eggplant

24

Use it with fish and shell fish stewed in coconut cream and greens.

Combine with garlic.

Use in sweet and sour, stews and curries.

Dried ground ginger is not a true flavour substitute, but if no other form is available, i.e. fresh or canned, use it in half the quantity of fresh ginger called for in a recipe.

TOK PISIN: Kawawar

Green or Half-Ripe Pawpaw: (Carica papaya)
(Papaya)
Green or half-ripe pawpaw has many uses as a vegetable. Use it similarly to melons and gourds.

Green pawpaw has high amounts of papain, a base for meat tenderizer. To tenderize meat, rub with papaya juice and leave to work into the meat as you would meat tenderizer.

Choose fruit that is well formed and firm. It should keep for several days when stored on a rack.

Peel and seed small young pawpaws and stuff with freshly grated coconut and boil in coconut cream until tender.

Peel and boil whole green or half-ripe pawpaws until tender, remove seeds and stuff with meat or vegetable mixtures and serve.

Partially cook whole pawpaw or halves; stuff with meat or vegetable mixtures and bake in a moderate oven.

Peel, section, and boil in salted water and serve with white sauce. Cheese can be added to the white sauce.

Boil green pawpaw and mash with a little butter, salt and pepper to taste.

pawpaw   Make into patties with a little flour and fry in butter until light brown.

Add to stews, soups, curries or casseroles.

Cut slightly green pawpaw into eight wedges. Take out the seeds but leave on the skin. Sprinkle with salt and pepper and bake at a moderate heat for 20 to 30 minutes.

Use green pawpaws in pickles.

25

Add grated green pawpaw to salads

TOK PISIN: popo, papaia

Pitpit: (*Setaria palmifolia, Saccharum edule*)
(Duruka)

Pitpit is a type of wild sugar cane with edible fruit resembling an unripe ear of maize which is found inside the tightly closed long light green leaves. The fruit is a whitish colour with a somewhat sponge-like texture. The stems of pitpit are used for light fences and walls. Some varieties of pitpit are referred to as Papua New Guinea asparagus. This is an apt name as pitpit, too, can be a most delicate vegetable when cooked carefully and correctly.

When buying pitpit choose stems with tightly furled buds. Use as soon after buying as possible. Before cooking stand the bundles up-right in a cool place. Pitpit will keep up to 24 hours and it freezes well.

To prepare pitpit, break off the section containing the pitpit bud carefully; remove the leaves and discard. Use only the edible bud.

Bake pitpit in its outer leaves in the oven or hot ashes; then peel and eat with salt and pepper and butter.

Remove the outer leaves from the pitpit; boil or steam and eat with butter or a cheese sauce or a white sauce.

Line an oven dish with foil, peel the pitpit and place in the dish; cover with thick coconut cream; and add salt, pepper and bits of butter. Close the foil and bake for 30 minutes in a moderate oven. Lime slices may be added with the salt and pepper.

Cook pitpit in the pot along with rice. It is especially good with coconut rice.

Steam pitpit; drain well. Serve with coconut cream or cheese sauce. Use cooked pitpit in salads marinated in French Dressing.

Do not remove all the leaves from the bud; bake in the oven until soft; remove and discard the leaves and use as above or serve hot with butter, salt and pepper. Cooking pitpit in the leaves preserves the flavor.

pitpit

Bake with the outside sheath on; remove and simmer the buds gently in coconut cream.

SEASONINGS: caraway seed, celery seed, salt, chili powder, dill, mint, mustard, paprika, savory

Pumpkin:
(Chinese marrow; Round, Bottle, Long Gourds, Snake Bean, Hauki, Luffa, Taroi, Squash)

Pumpkin comes in a wide variety of shapes and sizes from those that are long and thin to those that are round and squat. Try all the types you find in the market to discover your favorites.

Choose fruit which is young and firm; older fruit contains too many seeds and the flesh is spongy.

Pumpkins will keep for several days on racks.

To prepare, peel or scrape, cut into slices or dice.

Use in Papua New Guinean dishes with root vegetables but add much later as it cooks much more rapidly.

Boil and mash with thick coconut cream. Add a little chopped onion or grated coconut.

Steam or boil in salted water. Drain well.

Add ginger when boiling for a nice change of flavour.

Serve with white sauce or with flavoured sauce of cheese or tomato. Use in curries, stews and soup.

Choose medium sized fruit. Cut off top, scoop out centre and stuff with meat, vegetables, and rice mixtures.

Leave peel on, split in halves or quarters; score deeply; dot with butter, sprinkle with salt and pepper and bake at 375 F for 30 to 40 minutes.

Use in scones, break, or cake.

pumpkin

Substitute pumpkins for bananas or apple sauce in banana cake or apple sauce cake.

TOK PISIN: pamken

Taro Stalks: Choose the pinkish and white stalks near the root or leaf but not the middle. Do not use the dark stalks either.

27

To prepare taro stalks, cut in short lengths and peel off a thin layer of skin.

Taro stalks can be added to boiled, steamed or baked food or they can be eaten on their own.

Boil the stalks until tender in salted water or coconut cream. Serve with white sauce or miti (page 99).

FRUITS

*T*here is a wide variety of fruit grown in the various areas of Papua New Guinea with bananas, pawpaw, and pineapple available in most areas. This section contains a detailed description of the more commonly found fruits and brief descriptions of some of the other fruits.

Many tropical fruits are sweeter than those found in temperate climates and some have to be eaten several times before they become addictive.

Generally Papua New Guineans regard fruit as a snack food and eat most fruit fresh which is by far the best way nutritionally and taste-wise.

Eating Bananas: Eating bananas vary from a finger-length species to the long eating bananas most North Americans are familiar with. Many of the smaller varieties are very sweet.

Where the ridges on cooking bananas are quite sharp, eating bananas have no distinct ridges down the sides. Ripe bananas are pale greenish yellow to deep yellow in colour. Often very ripe bananas will have brown or black spots on their skin.

When eating bananas are ripe, all the starch is turned into sugars which are easily digested.

Hang banana bunches in cool dark places. If you cut the bunch down from the plant when the bottom rows are ripe the others will ripen gradually so that you will have fruit available for a longer period. Remember once a banana plant has born fruit it must be cut down so that a new tree can sprout. Banana plants can develop and mature in as little as 10 months in the correct conditions.

bananas

Hands of bananas can be kept on racks for 2 to 3 days. Do not store in the refrigerator.

28

As ripe bananas are easily digested, mashed bananas mixed with milk is used as a food for babies, invalids and old people.

Recipes from temperate climates for banana cakes and breads often fail in the tropics. Those included in this collection have been tried successfully.

Don't add ripe eating bananas to a pot of vegetables as it will make the mixture sappy and spoil it. Occasionally some dishes call for ripe eating bananas because of this property.

As bananas are a favorite fruit everywhere the list of recipes for bananas is endless. This collection only contains a small sample.

Boil eating bananas in their skins with water or peeled with coconut cream. If you like, add a little brown sugar to the liquid.

Peel ripe bananas and cut into halves and fry with bacon and eggs and tomatoes for breakfast, turning them over in the pan as soon as the bananas are golden brown. Do not cook too long or they will become too soft and burn.

Halve bananas, dip in a mixture of egg, salt and lemon juice and roll in breadcrumbs or cornflake crumbs. Deep fry for about two minutes. Serve with chicken or fish.

Dip small peeled bananas into Miracle Whip and roll in toasted coconut. Serve with lettuce.

Dredge thickly-sliced bananas with seasoned flour and fry in dripping or butter until delicately browned. Sprinkle with sugar and lemon juice. Serve as a savory or sweet.

Bake ripe bananas until their skins split (approximately 20 minutes); brush with butter; season with salt and pepper and serve as a savory.

Peel, place in a baking dish and sprinkle with sugar and lemon juice and dab with butter. Bake in a moderate oven for 20 minutes. Serve as a sweet.

mango

Mango: (*Mangifera indica*)   A sweet tropical fruit. The skin is smooth and usually turns from light green to greenish yellow to yellow or orange (often with splotches of scarlet) depending on ripeness. Some varieties of mango remain green outside when ripe. The stone inside is long and flat and the flesh when ripe is yellow, soft and juicy. Many of the mangoes in PNG tend to be stringy and not quite as pleasant to eat. In some areas, the larger less stringy varieties can be found. All mangoes are delicious even if stringy and are extra special because they are only available seasonally.

Usually this is during the hottest season.

Choose fruit with firm flesh. Avoid ripe fruit with a turpentine smell. Ripe mangoes can be stored on racks in a cool dark place for 2 days and green mangoes will keep longer.

If you want a tidy looking fruit, peel green and ripe mangoes with a knife. If you are not so concerned with the looks of the end product, ripe mangoes can quickly be peeled by separating the flesh from the skin with sharp pulls. A knife may be needed to start.

Don't leave the seed in green mangoes when cooking as it tends to be bitter Boil peeled whole or sliced ripe mangoes in coconut cream.

Boil unpeeled ripe mangoes in water. Add sugar or a syrup and use as a dessert.

Peel ripe fruit and use raw in fruit or vegetable salads.

Use ripe mangoes in pies and cakes similarly to peaches. Flavor with nutmeg, cinnamon or lemon.

Use green mangoes as apples in pies and cakes. Flavor with cinnamon and nutmeg.

Cook ripe or half-ripe fruit in water and sugar and make a puree for ice cream or a souffle.

Make a drink by combining grated mango with water, coconut cream and a little sugar.

Use green or half-ripe mangoes, in jams and jellies as mango juice contains plenty of pectin.

Use green, half-ripe or ripe fruits in chutney. Use green or half-ripe fruits in pickles.

Slice green mangoes thinly and eat with a mixture of salt, sugar and fresh chilies. Don't eat too many, though!

TOK PISIN: mango

fruits

Pawpaw: (Carica papaya)
(Papaya)

A cylindrical or pear shaped tropical fruit ranging from three to twenty inches in length and weighing up to ten pounds (5 kg). The skin is green and thin when unripe. When the fruit is ripe both the skin and flesh are orange yellow to deep orange with a mass of small blackish seeds in the center. The ripe flesh is sweet, with a slight musky taste. "Red" or "Solomons" pawpaw is reputed to be the best in PNG.

Many people don't like pawpaw the first time they try it but they usually develop a strong preference for this nutritious fruit.

Choose firm fruit. Large darker coloured spots may indicate that the fruit is over-ripe. Keep ripe pawpaws on racks for 1 to 2 days and up to 4 days under refrigeration.

Lemon and lime juice compliment the sweet taste of pawpaw and often make the fruit more palatable to Westernized tastes. Pawpaw tastes best when chilled.

As ripe pawpaw is easily digested, mashed pawpaw is a popular early baby food. Boil pawpaw cubes in coconut cream until tender.

Cut pawpaw in halves or quarters, remove seeds, flavor with lemon or lime and serve as a breakfast fruit.

Cut into cubes and add to salads or fruit cocktail.

Add small pieces to coleslaw.

Use for jam making as it contains a natural pectin.

Cooked pawpaw may be used in Jello but raw pawpaw stops gelatine from setting.

Make a drink using 2 cups mashed ripe pawpaw; 1 t. sugar; 2 cups water; milk or coconut water; and a little lemon juice.

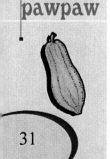

pawpaw

Combine scraped ripe pawpaw with freshly scraped coconut.

Place thinly sliced pawpaw in a pie dish and pour coconut cream mixed with sugar over it and bake in a moderate oven for 12 hours.

Combine cubed pawpaw with lemon juice and chilies. Toss lightly. Serve immediately or marinate for up to 2 hours before serving.

Part 1: General Information

Pawpaw takes on the flavor of other fruit easily so it can be used to supplement fruits such as rhubarb or blackberries in pies, jams etc. If you use pawpaw in this way, you can cut down on the amount of sugar.

Use pawpaw in pies and cakes similarly to peaches. Flavour with nutmeg or cinnamon.

TOK PISIN: popo, papaia

Pineapples: (_Ananas comosus_) There are two main types of pineapples here. Fleshy, juicy ones and smaller ones with rougher skins.

Choose fruit which is firm all over and check for soft spots which indicate that the fruit is beginning to decay. Pineapple that is ready to eat will have a sweet smell and the leaves in the stem will come out easily when you pull them sharply. Store pineapples on racks. They will keep for 2-3 days or longer in a refrigerator.

Remove the stem and peel off the outer skin with a sharp knife. If you keep a little flesh with the stem you can plant it in your garden and you should have another pineapple in two years. Pineapples develop more rapidly from suckers than tops.

After the pineapple is peeled you will have to remove the black eyes. Once you get the knack this job isn't as formidable as it appears. Cut narrow wedges 1 inch deep diagonally across the fruit following the pattern of the eyes. Serve raw in slices, wedges or cubes with the dense core removed.

Add to salads of all types.

Serve cooked with meat, grilled, or fried until golden brown.

Use in pickles and chutney.

Do not use in gelatine mixtures unless cooked.

Place slices in a baking dish, sprinkle with lemon juice, nutmeg, cinnamon and a little brown sugar. Bake 10 minutes at 400 F. Serve warm, shower with freshly grated or toasted coconut.

pineapple

Quarter, remove core and cut each quarter in three wedges. Melt 2 t. butter in a skillet. Add pineapple and sprinkle with brown sugar. Heat.

Place pineapple skins and cores in a saucepan. Just cover with water and boil for half an hour. Strain and add sugar for a drink.

TOK PISIN: ananas, painap

OTHER COMMONLY FOUND FRUITS

Custard Apple: A scaly textured fruit, greenish in colour and about the same size as an orange. Soft buds of sweet musky tasting fruit are enclosed under each scale. A seed is in the centre of each bud of fruit and can be eaten or discarded. This fruit is best eaten fresh.

Guava: A medium sized fruit, which can be eaten green or ripe. It changes from a light green colour when green to a light greenish yellow when ripe. Treat green guava as you would green mango. Use ripe guava raw or stewed with sugar. Puree as a sauce. Makes jelly or jam.

Lemons: Lemons are ripe when greenish yellow but may be used as limes when still green. Use lemons as juice in drinks flavored with sugar. Grate finely for flavoring. Makes sauce, marmalade. Sprinkle juice over bananas, avocados, pawpaw and cantaloupes. Remove all pips, which are very bitter before using.

Limes: Limes are green and greenish yellow when ripe. Use fresh juice to drink or to flavor other fruits. Also use it to flavor fish, veal, green vegetables, and fried rice. Use in pickles, jellies and marmalade. Combine with baking soda to replace baking powder.

Malay Apple: A small pinkish-white fruit shaped something like a green pepper. Some varieties are predominantly pink while others are predominantly white. The Malay apple has a subtle flavor which is not too pronounced. Usually it is eaten raw especially to quench thirst, and it can also be used in chutney and jelly.

Mandarin Oranges: Greenish orange when ripe. Use fresh juice or peeled fruit by itself or in fruit salad or vegetable salad. Makes excellent jelly.

guava

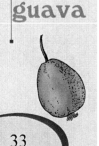

Oranges: Tropical oranges have coarse fibres separating segments and they have many large pips. Remove these with a sharp knife before eating. The juice is tart and usually requires sugar. Eat raw, or use in fruit salad and fruit drinks. Makes sauce and marmalade. Grate rind for flavoring.

33

Passionfruit: One variety of passionfruit has a tough black wrinkled skin when ripe. Another has a smooth skin and is deep orange in colour when ripe. Another is yellow to brownish, yellow with slightly wrinkled skin when ripe.

Use passionfruit raw by cutting in half and scooping out the pulp and seeds. The seeds are edible. Sprinkle over ice cream or fruit salad. Particularly good with bananas. Add to fruit drinks. Mix into cake icing.

Pomelo: A large grapefruit-shaped fruit with a thick fleshy skin that must be cut off with a strong knife. Separate the individual sections and remove the tough membrane and large seeds. Pomelos with pink flesh are much sweeter than the white-fleshed varieties.

Serve pomelo raw with sugar if necessary. Combine with avocado to form a fruit cocktail. Use in salads and in marmalade jam.

Rambutan: A pinkish hairy fruit growing in a cluster. Run a knife around the centre of the tough outer skin to remove the soft white fruit. Delicious when chilled.

Starfruit or Five Cornered Fruit: A light orange-colored. medium-sized fruit with five distinct ridges on its sides. When sliced cross-wise, star-shaped sections are produced. This fruit can tend to be sour so add sugar if necessary. Stew for sauces or add raw to salads. Use in marmalade.

Saporo: A large darkish brown fruit of no distinct shape. It has a soft sweet flesh which makes excellent juice for drinking. Use the juice in fruit salads, jellies and ice cream.

Part 1: General Information

rambutan

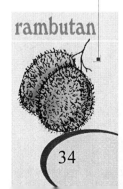

NUTS

Some nuts are eaten in a few areas in Papua New Guinea but they are even less important as a food than fruit. Nuts are always chewed as snack food and never added to dishes of food cooked for meals.

Several varieties of nuts can be found in various areas of the country. Experiment with them as snack foods and try adding them to fried dishes, stews and curries as a source of protein and a new taste. Remember nuts must be cooked to be valuable as a protein.

Okari Nuts: An elongated brown nut, about 1-¼ to 2 inches long, growing in pods in coastal areas. To be of full value nutritionally they should be cooked although they are very popular raw.

Roast whole in the oven or on hot ashes or slice thinly and fry or roast in a little oil. Don't salt until you want to eat them or they will become soggy very quickly.

Pandanus Nuts (or fruit): (*Pandanus* spp.)
This is the reddish-brown edible fruit of the pandanus. It grows in cluster and the individual nuts are pineapple shaped. They are popular roasted in the hot ashes of the fire. Usually they are sold already cooked.

TOK PISIN: marita

Peanuts: (*Arachis hypogaea*) Peanuts grow under the ground and are actually part of the root system of the plant.

They contain a high proportion of fat and body-building protein but must be cooked to release the protein. A diet of peanuts and sweet potatoes together, contain all necessary food groups and vitamins.

Peanuts are popularly eaten raw, boiled in their shells or roasted in hot ashes in their shells.

Add to stews and curries.

peanuts

Crush and add to baking and fried vegetables and meat.

To make peanut butter roast the peanuts but be careful not to brown too much. Put through a mincer, twice if necessary, add salt and oil to taste. Sugar too, if you like it sweet.

TOK PISIN: kasang galip

RECIPES

Part 2 – Traditional and Modern

FROM PAPUA NEW GUINEA

ABUS

CHICKEN

Chicken Pot (Adapted to Port Moresby)

one chicken cut into serving pieces
a little oil
kaukau
bunch of green onions
 pumpkin tips
cobs of corn
2 coconuts for cream salt to taste
curry powder to taste

1. Place chicken in the pot with a little oil if necessary.
2. Chop kaukau and place on top of chicken.
3. Coarsely chop green onion and add next.
4. Coarsely chop pumpkin tips and add next.
5. Peel and break corn to place on top of greens.
6. Squeeze coconut milk over the meat and vegetables to cover.
7. Cover and bring to a boil.
8. Cook gently for 30-40 minutes.
9. Add salt and curry powder.
10. Serve as a meal. You could separate the vegetables and meat for serving and place the liquid in a container to serve as a sauce or soup.

Chicken and Vegetables

butter for browning
1 chicken cut into serving pieces
1 coconut for cream
enough vegetables to serve 6 people: tapioca, yam, banana;
    pumpkin, kaukau, onions, etc.

1. Brown the chicken in a little butter in a heavy frying pan (electric if you have one).
2. Add peeled, washed and chopped vegetables to frying pan.
3. Cover with coconut cream.
4. Add a little salt, chopped onions and any seasoning to taste.
5. Cover and cook slowly until vegetables are tender, about half an hour.

Part 2: Traditional & Modern Recipes from PNG

Mumu in a Drum (Adapted from the Highlands)

an empty and clean 5 gallon drum
smooth stones to cover the bottom of the drum
large banana or other leaves
1 or 2 chickens
piece of pork
starchy vegetables
greens
2 or more coconuts for cream

1. Wash and peel the vegetables and coarsely chop or break into serving size pieces.
2. Wash and clean greens. Coarsely chop if they are very large.
3. Chop the chicken and pork into large pieces.
4. Grate coconut
5. Clean drum. If it has never been used for cooking before burn any possible residue.
6. Cover the bottom of the drum with rocks.
7. Place the banana leaves on top of the rocks.
8. Add root vegetables placing the longest cooking at the bottom.
9. Add pork pieces and then chicken pieces.
10. Place greens on top of the meat or vegetables.
11. Squeeze coconut cream over the food. Traditionally Highlanders don't use coconut cream but some of them living on the coast have developed a taste for coconut flavour. The more coconut cream you use the richer your food will be.
12. Cover all the food in the drum with banana leaves tucking the ends between the food and the side of the drum
13. Place the drum on a grate over an open fire and cook for two or three hours.
14. Take the food out of the drum and serve on clean banana leaves. Separate the meat from the vegetables.
15. Eat with your hands.

ALTERNATIVES:
1. Use a boiler such as those equipped behind many of the older admin houses. Place leaves, stones and food inside the boiler as you would inside a drum. Build the fire underneath.
2. Use a very large cooking pot over a gas or electric stove. This is a cleaner method but not as smoky tasting.

...abus

BULLY BEEF

Corned Beef (Medina High School Style)

    rice
    corned beef (one tin)
    tomatoes
    coconut cream

1. Cook the rice
2. Make layers of the rice, corned beef and tomatoes.
3. Pour enough coconut cream over the layers to dampen them all with the cream.
4. Bake until it is hot.

Corned Beef and Pumpkin (Milne Bay)

    1 bunch of pumpkin tips or other greens
    1 small pumpkin
    1 onion chopped
    1 tin bully beef
    1 coconut for cream
    salt to taste
    1 ½ cups water or enough to cover pumpkin

1. Bring water to boil in a medium sized saucepan.
2. Add pumpkin; cook until tender.
3. Add chopped pumpkin tips and cook 5-10 minutes.
4. Mash corned beef lightly and stir into the vegetables.
5. When the mixture is warmed throughout, squeeze coconut cream over it and continue cooking for 5-10 minutes.
6. Serve with coconut rice.

ALTERNATIVES:
1. If you have lots of coconuts use coconut cream for step 1.
2. Use thinly sliced or cubed fresh beef. Add before the pumpkin tips as fresh meat takes longer to cook than canned beef.
3. Use tinned fish instead of bully beef and add more ingredients for flavor such as curry powder or chillies.
4. Add pitpit shoots when you add the pumpkin.

Praim Corned Beef

Yu mas i gat:
    1 tin corned beef
    sampela poteito o rais

abus...

1 kiau
sol
gris
sampela anian

Wei bilong wokim:
1. Kukim rais o poteito pastaim. Taim poteito i kuk pinis paitim gut long fok.
2. Kapsaitim tin mit long wanpela dis na brukim gut long fok.
3. Katim anian liklik na tanim wantaim mit.
4. Brukim wanpela kiau na tanim wantaim mit tu.
5. Tanimm rais o poteito wantaim mit.
6. Putim gris long praipan na taim em i hat kapsaitim mit na poteito. Kukim long taim liklik inap i kamap braun long aninit long en.
7. Tainim bai em i kamap braun tu long hap sait.

Vegetables and Bully Beef

    1 tin bully beef
    bunch of pumpkin tips, chopped
    tomatoes, chopped or sliced thinly
    onions, chopped
    salt
    a little butter
    large (eating) taro leaves

1. Partly fry the washed and chopped vegetables until tender.
2. Add the bully beef and salt.
3. Mix the vegetables and bully beef thoroughly.
4. Remove from the stove and wrap in taro leaves.
5. Place on top of vegetables cooking in a large pot, or bake for 30 minutes in a moderate oven.
6. Serve with root vegetables cooked in coconut cream or rice.

FRESH BEEF

Morobe Meat Patties (PNG)

    500 gm minced steak
    ½ bunch spring onions, chopped with leaves
    ½ root fresh ginger, finely chopped
    1 large nambis pitpit, broken into small crumbs
    1 large capsicum, chopped
    2 cm stem of lemon grass, finely chopped
    3 hot chilies (optional)
    1 large or two medium eggs
    1/8 t. of spice bark from Lae market

½ t. black pepper
1 t. lemon juice
grated peel of half a lemon
salt to taste

1. Combine all ingredients and form into 10 balls.
2. Flatten and brown on both sides in coconut oil or drippings.
3. Reduce heat and cook through.
4. Serve with a salad of tomatoes, cucumber and sliced banana.

FRESH FISH

Baked fish in Coconut Milk

fish
coconut milk
salt
1 lemon (sliced or juice only)
1 onion, sliced
1 t. curry powder

1. Cut the fish in half or leave it whole if it is a small fish.
2. Placed fish in grease baking dish.
3. Add salt, onion, tomato, curry powder, lemon.
4. Pour in coconut milk.
5. Bake for 15 minutes or until the fish flakes when touched with a fork.

Baked Stuffed Fish

1 medium sized fish
1 cup bread crumbs, cooked rice or cooked mashed root vegetables
1 t. salt, pepper and/or chilies
2 tomatoes, sliced
1 onion, finely chopped
1 egg or a small quantity of milk or coconut cream
1 t. mixed herbs
1 t. chopped parsley
grated rind of one lemon (optional)

1. Remove the scales, eyes and internal parts of the fish.
2. Mix together all the other ingredients except the tomatoes.
3. Place tomato slices inside the fish.
4. Stuff the fish with the mixture. Tie or sew up the fish.
5. Place the fish in a shallow dish with a little water or wrap it in leaves.
6. Bake in the oven for about an hour depending on the size of the fish.

abus...

VARIATION:
Instead of putting the onion and tomatoes inside the fish, cut both into rings and arrange alternately along the back of the fish when half-cooked.

NOTE
Often, when fish bones are removed the flesh of the fish breaks into pieces. If so, sew or tie together or wrap firmly in leaves.

Fish Dish

2 fish
1 onion
2 tomatoes
2 coconuts
young taro leaves to cover fish
salt and pepper

1. Scale and clean fish. Cut into pieces if the fish is extra thick. Remove bones.
2. Wash young taro leaves carefully and remove ribs.
3. Squeeze coconut cream.
4. Cut onion into rings and slice tomatoes.
5. Put fish on layer of taro leaves in a baking dish.
6. Place onion rings and tomato slices in layers on top of the fish.
7. Cover with coconut cream and add salt and pepper.
8. Cover with more taro leaves.
9. Cover with more coconut cream.
10. Bake in a moderate oven for about ¾ hour.
11. Serve with boiled rice or root vegetables cooked in coconut milk.

VARIATION:
If you have no oven, place the fish in a bowl rather than a baking dish and stand the bowl in a saucepan of boiling water. Cover and steam until tender.

Fish Pot (Milne Bay)

1 whole fish
cleaned yam
taro
cooking banana
pumpkin tips
coconut for cream

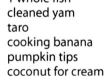

1. Boil yam, taro, and cooking bananas with coconut cream.
2. When boiling, add pumpkin tips and fish.
3. Simmer until the fish flakes when touched with the tip of a fork.
4. Serve as the main part of the meal or to accompany other dishes.

...abus

NOTE
You don't need to use all the root vegetables mentioned.

ALTERNATIVE METHOD:

Substitute pitpit for the root vegetables.

Fish and Vegetables (Central District)

> 1 large fish
> enough mixed fresh vegetables to serve four to six people: taro,
>   kaukau, hard bananas, ripe bananas, yam, pumpkin
> onions
> salt and pepper
> coconut cream
> water

1. Clean and scale the fish.
2. Prepare the vegetables and cut into serving pieces.
3. Place taro, kaukau, hard bananas in the bottom of the saucepan.
4. Place yam in the middle.
5. Place pumpkin and ripe bananas on top.
6. Add salt and pepper and chopped onion.
7. Cover the saucepan and bring to a boil.
8. When boiling add the fish.
9. Lower the heat and simmer until the vegetables are soft and the fish flakes.
10. Separate the fish and vegetables and place on separate serving dishes. Add a little of the liquid.
11. Pour the remainder of the liquid into a jug and serve as an accompanying soup with the meal.

One Pot Yam Fish Dish (Hula)

> 2 lb. fish: either one small fillet per person or one large fish
> 1 bunch spring onions
> 3 pieces of pitpit
> 1 bundle of pumpkin tips
> 1 bunch of aibika leaves
> 2 coconuts for cream
> 1 large yam
> 5 ripe cooking bananas
> 1 lb. fresh tomatoes
> 1 bundle of long green beans (optional)

1. Clean all leafy vegetables.
2. Scrape the coconut out of its shell.
3. Peel yam and bananas.

abus...

42

4. Scale fish if necessary.

5. Chop all ingredients into small sizes for quick, even cooking.

6. Place into a large saucepan and cover with squeezed coconut cream.

7. Cook over moderate heat until all ingredients are tender.

Vegetables and Greens Served with Fish (Rabaul)

> taro
> Chinese taro
> cooking bananas
> kaukau
> bunch of pumpkin tips
> bunch of aibika
> watercress
> bunch of long green beans
> spring onions
> 2 coconuts for cream
> salt to taste

1. Clean and chop vegetables.

2. Place taro, bananas and kaukau in a pot and cover with coconut cream.

3. Add chopped onion and tomato.

4. Boil gently until tender.

5. If adding greens, parboil for 5-10 minutes and add to other vegetables after they have been cooking for about half an hour.

FISH:

1. Clean and wash and chop the greens.

2. Cover with water and partly cook for about 10 minutes.

3. Drain greens and return to pot.

4. Cut fish in chunks and add to pot.

5. Squeeze coconut cream to cover fish and greens.

6. Cook gently over moderate heat until the fish is tender.

7. Add a pinch of salt.

ALTERNATIVE: Use chicken in place of fish.

SHELL FISH

Crab and Greens (Central District)

> 1 female crab (fat, heavy, wide flap in front)
> 1 onion, chopped finely
> 1 tomato, chopped finely
> 1 bunch of greens, chopped finely
> 1 coconut for cream

Part 2: Traditional & Modern Recipes from PNG

1. Boil the crab in its shell.
2. Remove the meat from the cooked crab.
3. Break the crab meat into small pieces and combine it with the finely chopped vegetables.
4. Squeeze thick coconut cream over the meat and vegetable mixture.
5. Cook gently until the greens are tender.

Hula Crab and Taro (Central District)

1 large crab
1 bundle spring onions
1 lb. fresh tomatoes
1 bundle of pumpkin tips
1 large taro or tapioca or other root vegetable
2 coconuts for cream
lemon juice

CRAB:
1. Cook the crab in boiling water and remove all flesh.
2. Clean and chop the onions, tomatoes and pumpkin tips.
3. Place the crab and vegetables in a pot and cover with coconut cream. Add a pinch of salt and lemon juice.
4. Cook over low heat for 20 to 30 minutes.
5. Serve with taro.

TARO:
1. Cook separately in a pot until tender. Use water or coconut milk.
2. Peel, cut into serving pieces.
3. Sprinkle with salt and pepper.

Steamed Crab (Central District)

1 female crab (fat, heavy, wide flap in front)
1 onion, chopped finely
1 tomato, chopped finely
grated coconut
2 bunches of greens

1. Break the shell while the crab is still alive.
2. Scrape out the guts but not the meat; a greenish to yellow-red color fairly runny.
3. Combine the crab's insides with the chopped onion, tomato and grated coconut.
4. Stuff the above mixture into the shell of the crab.
5. Close the shells for steaming.

6. Place prepared greens in a pot and cover with coconut cream.
7. When simmering place the crab on top of the greens.
8. Cover the pot and cook gently until the meat is tender.

ALTERNATIVE: Use root vegetables instead of greens. Add the crab a little later.

Kaukau Crayfish

fresh crayfish, boiled in sea-water, cracked and meat taken out
½ kilo kaukau
1 bunch spring onions
½ kilo tree tomatoes
small bunch peanuts
40 grams (generous spoonful) butter

1. Cook kaukau and chop small.
2. Slice cray meat, chop onions small, slice tree tomatoes.
3. Lightly roast peanuts and remove from shells.
4. Melt butter and warm all ingredients in it, mixing gently.
5. Turn mixture into cray shell halves to serve.

TINNED FISH

Fish Cakes

1 large tin of fish
4 medium kaukau
1 T. butter
1 T. milk
1 egg or substitute
salt and pepper to taste
1 T. lemon or lime juice
flour
bread crumbs (optional)

1. Boil kaukau and mash.
2. Add flaked fish, then heated butter and milk.
3. While still warm stir in egg yolk beaten with salt and pepper and lemon juice.
4. Shape into 10-12 patties and coat lightly with flour.
5. Dip in egg white beaten, and roll in bread crumbs. (optional step)
6. Fry in hot oil or fat until golden brown.

Part 2: Traditional & Modern Recipes from PNG

Kol Pis Na Rais

Yu mas i gat:
   2 kap rais
   1 tin pis (bikpela)
   1 kiau
   1 muli
   sol

We bilong wokim:
1. Kukim rais wantaim sampela sol pastaim.
2. Kisim wara bilong muli na tainim wantaim rais.
3. Putim rais long wanpela dis na putim long ples kol.
4. Boilim kiau inap long 15 minit. Kwiktaim putim long kol wara na rausim
   skin bilong en. Kisim waitpela hap long kiau na katim.
5. Opim tin pis na kapsaitim pis long siv inap ol wara i ken ron i go. Yusim fok
   na brukim pis gut.
6. Tainim pis wantaim rais na putimm olgeta i go long wanpela dis.
7. Putim hap kiau i yelo i go long siv na yusim spun long sikarapim antap
   long rais na pis.

Pis Pai

Yu mas i gat:
   1 bikpela tin pis
   1 kiau
   4 anian
   8 spun margarine (bata)
   4 kap susu
   Sol
   sampela poteito

We bilong wokim:
1. Rausim skin bilong potato. Boilim poteito. Taim em i malumalum paitim
   em long fok.
2. Putim kiau long sospan i gat wara long en na boilim inap long 15 minit.
   Kwiktaim putim kiau long kol wara. Taim em i kol rausim skin bilong en na
   katim liklik.
3. Kapsaitim pis long wanpela dis na brukim pis gut. Putim kiau
   wantaim pis.
4. Putim margarine long sospan na hatim. Putim plaua na tainimm
   wantaim. Kapsaitim liklik susu na tainim na kapsaitim liklik moa i
   go olsem inap yu tainim pinis olgeta susu.
5. Katim anian liklik tru na tanim wantaim sos.
6. Tanim pis na kiau wantaim sos na putim long wanpela dis.
7. Putim poteito antop long pis. Putim long aven na hatim inap
   poteito i kamap braun.

abus...

KUMU

Bugandi Egg-Drop Soup (PNG)

1 bunch of choko or pumpkin shoots
1 bunch spring onions
12 leaves local spinach (stalks removed)
4 eggs
salt to taste
½ gm. pepper, freshly ground

1. Boil or pressure-cook choko shoots until tender enough to crush for juice for stock.
2. Add water if necessary to make up to one liter and add salt to taste.
3. Chop spring onions (including tops) and spinach leaves and add to boiling stock.
4. Simmer for seven minutes while lightly beating eggs and pepper.
5. Stir stock while slowly adding beaten egg in a thin stream.
6. Serve immediately.

Dish of Greens (Papuan Coast)

bunch of aibika
bunch of pumpkin tips
bunch of any other available greens
1 onion
2 tomatoes
bunch of long green beans
2 long green eating bananas
2 muli (or lemons)
pinch of salt

1. Smoke bananas in skins in hot ashes in the fire or boil in their skins until tender when pricked with a fork.
2. Wash greens and parboil in approximately ½ cup of water for 5-10 minutes. Drain.
3. In a saucepan place slices of banana, chopped onion, sliced tomatoes, and greens.
4. Cover with coconut milk and add young chopped muli and a pinch of salt.
5. Boil gently until greens are tender. (Approximately half an hour).
6. Serve as part of a meal.

...kumu

Part 2: Traditional & Modern Recipes from PNG

ALTERNATIVES:

1. Add pitpit.
2. Use onion juice in place of chopped muli
3. Add a couple of young taro leaves, chopped finely.

Fish and Greens (Hula)

fish
aibika leaves
pumpkin tips
long green beans
2 coconuts for cream
2 tomatoes
1 onion
salt

1. Clean fish, chop into serving-sized pieces and place into a pot.
2. Squeeze coconut cream over the fish until it is well covered. Remember you will be adding the vegetables.
3. Place the fish and coconut cream over medium heat.
4. Add the chopped green beans.
5. Roughly chop the greens, parboil, and add to the pot.
6. Add the chopped onion.
7. Add the thinly sliced tomato.
8. Simmer until the fish flakes and the greens are tender.
9. Add a pinch of salt.
10. Serve hot in bowls or coconut shells.

Shell-Fish and Greens (Milne Bay)

mangrove clams
1 fresh ginger-root (or to taste)
1 bunch ota fern
1 bunch pumpkin tips
1 bunch aibika
1 coconut for cream
salt to taste

1. Boil shellfish with enough water to cover.
2. Grate coconut. Parboil the greens for 5-10 minutes.
3. When the clams are cooked (the shells will open), remove the meat. Reserve the stock.
4. Combine the fish and stock and squeeze the coconut milk over them.
5. Bring to a boil and add chopped or sliced ginger-root and greens.
6. Simmer until the greens are cooked. (about 15 minutes)
7. Add a little salt and serve with coconut rice.

Part 2: Traditional & Modern Recipes from PNG

kumu...

NOTE: It is not necessary to use all the types of greens listed. You may also substitute others if those listed are not available. Do try to include the ferns if at all possible.

Stuffed Green Pawpaw (Papuan Coast)

> 3 or more small green pawpaws
> pumpkin tips, aibika or any other greens
> 1 onion
> salt
> pepper
> 1 coconut for cream

1. Peel the pawpaws and remove the tops.
2. Boil in water until tender when pricked with a fork. Don't boil them too long or they will become soggy.
3. Remove pawpaw from the boiling water, drain and carefully scrape out any seeds.
4. Wash the greens and chop finely.
5. Cook the greens gently in a little water until tender.
6. Drain the water from the greens.
7. Squeeze the thick coconut cream over the greens. (Do not add water to the grated coconut when making this cream)
8. Add chopped onions, salt and pepper, and any other seasonings to the greens. Add coconut cream. Mix well. You may want to stir-fry the mixture very quickly to blend well.
9. Stuff the cooked pawpaw and serve.
10. If desired, heat in the oven before serving.

VARIATION:

1. Stuff the pawpaws with the stuffing for the sago and coconut pancakes.
2. Use cooking onions raw or gently fry the chopped onion and cook with the greens.
3. Stuff large pawpaws with meat or vegetables and bake.

...kumu

STAPLES

RICE

Coconut Rice

> 2 cups rice
> 1 t. salt
> 3 ½ cups coconut milk

1. Bring coconut milk to a boil with salt.
2. Using a wooden spoon, stir the milk to make sure that the milk does not curdle.
3. Wash the rice. Put it in the boiling milk. Put the lid on.
4. When the milk is boiling again, lower the heat and leave it like that until it is cooked.
5. Another method is to put the rice and coconut milk in the oven at about 200 F.

Pumpkin Rice

1. Cook one and a half cups rice in either coconut milk or water until done.
2. Mash one cup of cooked pumpkin.
3. Blend rice and pumpkin then serve with chicken and vegetables.

Yellow Rice

> 3 cups coconut milk
> 1 t. laoli (yellow coloring or turmeric)
> 1 cup rice
> 1 t. salt

1. Bring coconut milk, salt and coloring to a boil.
2. Wash rice, drain and add to boiling coconut milk.
3. When it begins to dry up, turn heat down to low so the steam dries the rice up.

ROOT VEGETABLES

Root Vegetables Cooked in Coconut Cream (Rabaul)

> one taro
> one Chinese taro
> two tapioca
> pile of kaukau

staples

one medium yam
two coconuts for cream
one onion, chopped
pinch of salt

1. Peel, chop vegetables.
2. Place in a saucepan in order of cooking time: taro, Chinese taro, tapioca, kaukau, yam.
3. Add water to level of vegetables and boil.
4. When almost cooked, squeeze cream from two coconuts into pot.
5. Add chopped onion and a pinch of salt.
6. Continue cooking gently until vegetables are tender.
7. Serve as part of a meal.

ALTERNATIVES

1. Only use some of the root vegetables listed here.
2. Add cooking bananas after the tapioca.
3. Add English potatoes after the kaukau.
4. Add pumpkin when you add the coconut cream.
5. Add fish or greens when you add the coconut milk. DON'T add both.

SAGO

Dia (Sago, Banana and Coconut Cream, Motu Style)

This is a very rich dish and may be used as an entree, main dish or sweet.

4 old coconuts for cream
2 cups mashed ripe bananas (mix cooking and eating bananas)
½ to 1 cup sago
8 rinsed banana or canna leaves
string
salt
water
sugar

1. Mash the bananas to make up 2 cups. A mixture of cooking and eating bananas will make this dish soft and sweet.
2. Add sago flour and mix. You will have to experiment with the amount of sago that you prefer.
3. Add about 2 cup uncooked coconut milk and mix well.
4. Cut the banana leaves in half and dip into hot water for easier handling.
5. Place about ¼ cup of this mixture onto the centre of a washed banana leaf.
(If there is any juice in the bowl put a little of it on the leaf first.)

staples

Part 2: Traditional & Modern Recipes from PNG

Make the parcels any size. Sometimes all the mixture is put on one big leaf.
6. Wrap the leaf closed lengthwise, then fold over the two ends so that the parcel looks like a rectangle.
7. Tie with the string lengthwise and crosswise.
8. Repeat until the mixture is all used up.
9. Bring enough water to cover the stuffed leaves and bring to a boil.
10. Place the parcels in the boiling water and cover the pot with 2 or 3 flat banana leaves.
11. Gently boil for 40 minutes to an hour depending on the size of the parcels. Make sure the water doesn't boil off.
12. When cooked, take the special dish out of the leaves and serve covered with coconut cream.

Coconut Cream (Dia)

1. Grate coconuts and place in a bowl with one cup of water per coconut. (2 cups for 4 nuts)
2. Squeeze several times so that the water really mixes in.
3. Add a pinch of salt and ½ t. sugar for each coconut. Mix well.
4. Put cream in a saucepan and cook slowly over very low heat for up to one hour. Stir occasionally.

VARIATION:

Ketara: The sago and banana bundles are prepared the same way but they are served with oil instead of cream.

1. Grate the coconuts and place in a bowl with 1 cup of water for 2 cups of shredded coconut.
2. Squeeze several times so that the water really mixes in.
3. Put cream in a saucepan and bring to a boil.
4. Boil gently until clear. Stir occasionally so that it doesn't burn.

Daru Style

1. Use short fat yellow cooking bananas only.
2. Squeeze banana flesh with hands until all the lumps are gone.
3. Add a little uncooked coconut cream to the mashed bananas.
4. Powder a handful of sago flour between your hands and add to mixture.
5. Use three layers of banana leaves to make a boat.
6. Place a little raw coconut cream in the leaves. Put over all the surface in the same way as you would grease a cake pan, only wetter.
7. Place the banana–sago mixture in the center of the leaves.

staples

Part 2: Traditional & Modern Recipes from PNG

8. Pull up sides, gather in a bunch at the top and tie by winding string around top gather. Loop the string over the bottom in several places.
9. Place it up to the top tie in a pot of boiling water.
10. Cook for approximately one hour and a quarter.
11. Take from water, drain and untie to remove special dish.
12. Serve in coconut oil as in Ketara.

Sago Dumplings in Aibika Leaves (Milne Bay)

> 1 bunch aibika
> equal quantities of coconut and sago
> 2 chicken cubes
> coconut cream
> water
> pinch of salt

1. Wash aibika leaves and cut off from main stalk.
2. Put sago and scraped coconut into bowl and work until a moist but not wet consistency is reached (about a dry scone dough consistency)
3. Roll into small balls and flatten.
4. Wrap each patty in an aibika leaf.
5. Put coconut cream, water and chicken cubes into saucepan and bring to a boil.
6. Place dumplings, one at a time, gently into liquid and add a little salt.
7. Simmer until cooked and serve hot (about 10-15 minutes). If you're not sure if they're done remember that overcooking is better than under-cooking.

NOTE - These dumplings are very nice served cold, also.

Sago Dumplings

> 1 pound ripe bananas
> 1 pound sago powder
> 1 coconut for cream
> salt to taste
> clean banana leaves

1. Mix bananas and sago with your hands. Roll into balls.
2. Heat banana leaves in the fire to make them soft.
3. Wrap the rolls in banana leaves.
4. Bring the coconut cream to a boil, add salt and sago parcels.
5. Cook for 15 minutes.
6. Drain and unwrap the parcels.
7. Serve with fish.

Sago Pancakes (Milne Bay)

equal quantities of scraped coconut and sago

1. Place sago and scraped coconut into a bowl and work until a moist but not wet consistency is reached. (about a dry scone dough consistency)
2. Roll into small balls and flatten with your hands into thin patties.
3. Heat a heavy, ungreased frying pan to a medium heat.
4. Press one patty onto the surface of the pan until it is very thin. As the pancake cooks it will gradually stick together but you must keep pressing on the patty to keep it thin. (fat pancakes are leathery).
5. Brown on both sides. When cooked spread with butter and serve as it is or serve with a stuffing.

Stuffing for Sago Pancakes

bunch of ota fern
chopped onion
1 tin of-bully beef
A little butter

1. Remove small leaves from fern.
2. Separate bully beef with fork.
3. Fry chopped onion in a small amount of butter.
4. When the onion is soft and golden coloured, add bully beef. Stir-fry for 1 minute.
5. Add ferns and stir-fry just until ferns are heated throughout.

ALTERNATIVE:

1. Spread pancakes with jam or jelly.
2. Spread pancakes with sweetened condensed milk.

Sago Porridge

2 hands ripe bananas
5 cups sago

1. Mash bananas and put into a saucepan.
2. Sprinkle in sago and stir over a low heat for 10 minutes or until it is a porridge-like consistency.
3. Serve with rich coconut cream.

Part 2: Traditional & Modern Recipes from PNG

staples

54

Wuwu Sago

2 cups sago, sifted
1 cup mashed ripe banana
1 cup shredded coconut
1 teaspoon curry powder
1 teaspoon cinnamon
2 T. evaporated milk
1 egg
a little fat
1 ¼ cups grated cheese

1. Set oven at 350 F.
2. Mix all ingredients in a bowl to get a soft dough. Reserve cheese and cup shredded coconut.
3. Grease a baking tray.
4. Put mixture in the baking tray. Bake.
5. Remove from stove when cooked. (light brown on top)
6. Top with grated cheese and coconut seasoned with cinnamon.

Baked Sago Pudding

1 hand ripe banana
3 cups grated coconut
6 cups sago

1. Mash bananas in a large bowl.
2. Add grated coconut and sago and mix well with your hands. If the mixture is too dry, add a little coconut cream.
3. Place some clean bananas in the bottom of a baking tin.
4. Add mixture and cover with another clean banana leaf.
5. Bake in a moderate oven for 30 minutes. It will be brown when done.

TAPIOCA

Akinisi Dumplings

1 large tapioca root
shredded coconut from a young coconut

1. Grate tapioca and combine with the shredded coconut to form a doughy substance.
2. Form balls from the mixture and drop in boiling water until cooked.

NOTE: If you have trouble keeping the balls together try wrapping them in leaves before cooking. You could try either aibika leaves or soft banana leaves.

staples

Steamed Cassava

> 1 large tapioca root
> sugar to taste

1. Grate tapioca and combine with sugar.
2. Wrap in a banana leaf and tie.
3. Bake in fire or oven until cooked.

Tapioca Cream Squares

> tapioca (any amount)
> coconut (any amount)

1. Peel the tapioca, wash well and grate finely.
2. Scrape coconuts. For 5 coconuts use 1 cup of water.
3. Squeeze the coconut to make a thick cream.
4. Bring the cream to a boil. Boil rapidly until the oil is clear and the cream settles on the bottom of the pan. (Reserve some of the raw cream).
5. Pour out the oil. Scrape out the cream on to a plate.
6. Mix a little raw coconut cream with the grated tapioca.
7. Wrap the tapioca in clean leaves. Immerse gently in a pot of boiling water and cook for 35-45 minutes.
8. Remove parcels and drain.
9. Unwrap the parcels unless you have used edible leaves for wrappings.
10. Cut the parcels into squares and split in the middle, spread the cooked cream in the middle of the split squares.
11. Arrange the squares on a plate and pour coconut oil over them.
12. Serve hot or cold as an entree or sweet.

Tapioca Pudding (Sepik Feast Dish)

> 4 freshly scraped coconuts
> 2 cups water
> young banana leaves for wrapping
> white tapioca
> 2 ½ cups sugar

1. Boil coconut milk rapidly to make oil. (approximately 1 hour)
2. Peel the tapioca and grate.
3. Squeeze the juice out of the grated tapioca by placing it inside a cheesecloth and turning the cloth tighter and tighter.
4. Save the pulp and loosen it up with your fingers. Add a little fresh coconut cream and a pinch of salt to make a moist paste. It must not be so wet that it loses its shape.
5. Wrap the mixture in banana leaves. Close ends and tie.

Part 2: Traditional & Modern Recipes from PNG

staples

6. Cook in boiling water for about 1 hour.

7. Unwrap and cut into 1 inch cubes, after they have been cooled. (Can keep for 2 days without going bad).

8. Place sugar in a frying pan and place over low heat to melt until brown.

9. Add the sugar to the coconut oil mixture and stir and heat.

10. When serving place 6 or 7 chunks of pudding on a banana leaf and cover well with the coconut oil and sugar sauce.

Yam Crisps (Port Moresby)

yams (white yams with smooth skins are the best)
oil for deep-fat frying

1. Wash and peel the yams.

2. Use a potato peeler to slice thinly.

3. Soak in water to remove starch.

4. Dry slices on paper.

5. Deep-fry until crisp.

6. If your yam crisps become soggy, dry in the oven.

OTHER

Coconut-Keik Liklik

1 kap suga
1 kap plaua
1 kap pulap pulap long coconut yu sikirapim pinis
2 tispun baking powder
skin na wara blong wanpela muli (skin yu mas sikrapim pastaim)

Tanim ol samting, na putim liklik keik long kapa na putim long stove i hat. I mas stap nabaut 20 minit.

Mage (Ripe) Banana with Coconut Cream (Central District)

2 bananas for one person
4 coconuts
3 T. sugar or to taste
1 cup water

1. Peel the bananas and cook in pot with water and some syrup.

2. Boil slowly for 30 minutes.

3. Scrape coconuts, add water, squeeze out all the juice and bring, very slowly nearly to a boil. Add sugar during this period and stir occasionally. It must never come to a full boil.

others

Part 2: Traditional & Modern Recipes from PNG

4. Place a spoon in the pot and if the spoon is coated with cream remove the mixture from the stove. There should be thick lumps of cream formed on top of the mixture.
5. Place two bananas on each plate and spread the cream on the bananas.
6. Serve hot or cold.

Mashed Pumpkin and Coconut (Sepik)

    pumpkin
    coconut
    salt

1. Peel the pumpkin and cut into pieces for cooking.
2. Boil the pumpkin until tender in salted water or coconut milk.
3. Mash the pumpkin. If you have boiled the pumpkin in water mash it with thick coconut cream squeezed directly from grated coconut. If you have boiled the pumpkin in coconut milk use some of the cooking liquid for mashing.
4. Add grated coconut to mashed pumpkin. This can be gratings left over from squeezing or it can be freshly grated coconut.
5. Shape into balls or oblong patties and roll in grated coconut.
6. Serve hot or cold.

ALTERNATIVE:

1. Use sweet orange kaukau.
2. Mash any root vegetable with thick coconut cream but don't roll in grated coconut.

Patrol Stew (Highlands Style)

1. In a large saucepan put about 2 inches of water with salt and bring to a boil.
2. Peel and slice one medium kaukau per person and add to boiling water.
3. Prepare a combination of available vegetables such as beans, green onions, peas, carrots, cabbage, tomatoes so that there is enough for the number of people to be fed.
4. Add to kaukau in the saucepan along with ¼ to ½ cup of rice
5. When everything is nearly cooked, add one tin of meat or fish. Stir in well and cook for a few minutes.

NOTE: If using tomatoes, add a bit of sugar to cut the tartness of them.

others

58

LOCAL INGREDIENTS
Part 3 – Recipes using

Pitpit in Coconut Cream

> 10-12 pitpit depending on size
> 1 tomato
> 1 onion
> 2 coconuts for cream
> 1 and a ½ cups of water for making coconut cream

1. Prepare pitpit by peeling and cutting into serving sized pieces.
2. Chop onion and tomato.
3. Place pitpit and onion in a saucepan and squeeze coconut cream over them.
4. Boil until pitpit is tender.
5. Add tomato and continue cooking for 2-5 minutes.
6. Serve with other dishes as part of a meal.

Fruit salad

> 2 painap
> 8 banana
> 2 liklik pawpaw
> 2 muli
> 1 pint wara (hap liter)
> 3-4 teibalspun suga

Pastaim katim painap i kamap liklik i go long wanpela dis. Orait, yu katim liklik banana tu i go antap long painap.

Bihain katim pawpaw olsem tu, i go wantaim. Nau kisim wara i go wantaim sugar olsem wara blong muli. Tanim gut, na dispela samting i go antap long prut inap wara i haitim prut gut.

ABUS

BEEF

Beef and Spinach in Coconut Milk

...abus

> 2 lb. beef
> ½ t. ginger, fresh or powdered
> 2 T. oil
> 1 and a ½ t. salt
> 2 cups water
> ½ lb. spinach
> 2 T. butter

¾ cup coconut milk

1. Cut the meat in 12 inch squares; toss with ginger.
2. Heat the oil in a skillet; lightly brown the meat in it.
3. Add 1 t. salt and the water.
4. Cover and cook over low heat for 30 minutes or until tender.
5. Drain when cooked.
6. While the meat is cooking, sauté the spinach in the butter with the remaining salt for 10 minutes.
7. Add the meat and coconut milk to the spinach. Heat and serve.
8. Serves 4.

ALTERNATIVES:

1. Use Chinese spinach or water spinach.
2. Use young taro leaves but make sure the ribs are removed or there will be a bitter taste.

Muhogo Tamu (Beef and Tapioca Stew-East Africa)

1 lb. tapioca, peeled and cut into inch cubes
½ lbs. lean boneless beef, trimmed and cubed
1 T. salt
Freshly ground black pepper
¼ cup peanut or vegetable oil
1 cup finely chopped onions
1 T. Turmeric
2 mediums sized firm ripe tomatoes, cut into wedges
1 cup water
1 cup coconut cream
3 T. finely chopped fresh hot chilies
3 T. finely chopped fresh coriander (parsley or celery leaves)

1. Boil tapioca in lightly salted water for 30 minutes or until tender but still intact.
2. Sprinkle the meat on all sides with the salt and a few grindings of pepper.
3. Brown the beef, a few pieces at a time, in the oil. Transfer to a plate.
4. Add the onions to the fat remaining in the pan and cook for about 5 minutes or until they are soft and translucent.
5. Add the turmeric and stir for 1 minute.
6. Return the beef and the liquid that has accumulated around it to the pan. Add the tomatoes and water, and stir gently until the ingredients are well combined.
7. Bring to a boil over high heat and reduce the heat to low.
8. Simmer partly covered for about 1 hour or until the beef is tender.
9. Combine the coconut milk, chilies and coriander and stir into the stew.

staples

60

10. Add the tapioca and turn it about gently until it is evenly coated with cooking liquid.

11. Simmer partially covered for about 10 minutes longer, until the tapioca is heated through. Taste for seasoning.

12. Serve at once.

NOTE: Use a large heavy pot. If you use a frying pan for the first steps you eventually will have to transfer everything to a larger pot.

CHICKEN

Chicken Rou Rou Casserole (Fiji)

2 lb. chicken, deboned
Juice of lemon or lime
Seasoned flour
2 cups oil
Thick coconut cream (2 coconuts or more)
Approximately 1 and a ½ lb. of rou rou (taro leaves)
Two medium sized onions, chopped
2 or 3 tomatoes, sliced
Salt
Pepper
Chili

1. Cut the chicken into 1 inch pieces.
2. Marinate in lemon or lime juice plus ¼ cup of oil seasoned with salt and pepper for several hours.
3. Drain, roll in seasoned flour, and fry in 4 cup of hot oil until golden brown.
4. Prepare two cups of thick coconut cream. Season with one t. salt, a ¼ t. pepper and one finely chopped chili (or to taste).
5. Wash the rou rou leaves, removing the stems and coarse veins.
6. Place a layer of leaves in a casserole, cover with chicken pieces and sprinkle with onion.
7. Pour a little of the coconut cream over the chicken.
8. Repeat layers, making sure that the leaves are used for the last layer.
9. Place the sliced tomatoes on top of the last layer of leaves.
10. Cover the casserole and bake for 40 to 50 minutes at 350 F.
11. Serve with pieces of lemon or lime.

Chicken and Spinach in Coconut Cream (South Pacific)

2 and a ½ lb. chicken
2 T. oil

2 t. salt
¼ cup coconut cream
3 T. butter
½ lb. spinach

1. Debone the chicken and cut into cubes.
2. Heat the oil in a skillet and brown the chicken.
3. Add 12 t. salt and 4 cups coconut cream. Cover and cook over low heat for 20 minutes.
4. While the chicken is cooking, melt the butter in a saucepan; add the spinach and remaining salt.
5. Cover and cook over low heat for 15 minutes.
6. Add the chicken with the remaining coconut milk; bring to a boil and serve.

ALTERNATIVES:

1. Use chicken pieces rather than cubes.
2. Use Chinese spinach or water spinach.
3. Use young taro leaves but make sure the ribs are removed or there will be a bitter taste.

Hot Chicken Curry (Indonesia)

1 small chicken, jointed or pieces
2 T. peanut oil
1 onion, chopped
2 cloves garlic, crushed to a pulp
4 T. peanut butter
2 t. salt
1 pint coconut cream
2 T. flour
2-3 t. Indonesian-style curry powder
2 lemon or lime leaves

1. Heat the oil and gently fry the onion to soften.
2. Stir in curry powder. Add peanut butter and salt. Stir in flour and cook well.
3. Gradually stir in the coconut milk and keep stirring until the sauce boils.
4. Add chicken pieces and lemon or lime leaves. Simmer gently for two hours.

NOTE:

1. This dish is best made the day before it is eaten.
2. Fish or meat can replace the chicken.
3. Cooked jointed chicken can be used. This reduces the final cooking time to 20 minutes, but the finished flavor is not quite as good.

staples

4. Indonesian style curry powder:
2 T. chili powder
1 T. ground cumin
1 T. turmeric
1 T. ground coriander
1 T. ground ginger

Malay Curry

4 cloves garlic
Thumb-size piece fresh ginger
1 cup Malaysian curry powder (see note)
3 lb. chicken, cut up
¼ cup of peanut or other vegetable oil
1 large onion, chopped
1 large bay leaf
1 coconut for cream (make about 32 oz.)
½ T. salt

1. Peel and cut up garlic and ginger. Put in a mortar along with curry powder. (Add 1 tsp. crushed chilies if you want a hot curry.) Add a few drops cold water and pound with pestle; add more water drop by drop as needed, until a thick paste is formed. (If you don't have a mortar and pestle chop both ginger and garlic as fine as possible and mix and mash with curry powder and water until as smooth as possible.)

2. Rub chicken pieces with some of the curry mixture to give them a little coating.

3. Heat oil in a large skillet, as heavy as possible. Add onion and bay leaf and cook gently, stirring, until onion is lightly browned around the edges.

4. Add a little of the coconut cream. Stir in the remaining curry mixture.

5. Add chicken pieces and turn them over in the mixture to coat well and fry gently, adding a little of the coconut milk every 3 or 4 minutes, until chicken is lightly browned. This should take about 15 minutes and you will use about a cup of coconut milk.)

6. Add salt and all the remaining coconut cream.

7. Cover and simmer over very low heat until chicken is tender and part of the milk is cooked away, about 45 minutes.

...abus

NOTE:
Malaysian curry powder has lemon grass and cumin as flavoring. It is available in tins here. If you can't find it, use regular Indian curry powder, a pinch of cumin and a thick slice of lemon with the juice squeezed out. Add the cumin to the curry powder but add the lemon to the curry when you are adding the salt and remaining coconut cream just before the final simmering.

Part 3: Recipes Using Local Ingredients

FISH

Curried Barramundi

4 T. oil
Small piece of fresh ginger, chopped
1 large onion, thinly sliced
2 whole cloves garlic
½ T. ground chili powder
Coconut milk, about 2 and a ½ cups (from 1 coconut)
2 t. curry
powder
½ t. salt
1 T. sugar
2 cup cubed pineapple
1 tomato peeled and diced
1 lb. fresh or frozen barramundi fillets, slightly rubbed with salt (any other white fleshed fish will do)
Chopped fresh coriander, if available
Lemon juice

1. Heat the oil in a skillet and add the ginger, onion, garlic and ground chili.
2. Fry for about 5 minutes or until onions are lightly browned.
3. Add 2 cups coconut milk and bring just to a boil. Simmer 2 minutes.
4. Add curry powder, salt and sugar. Stir-fry over low heat for 10 minutes.
5. Stir in remaining coconut milk, and bring just to a boil.
6. Add pineapple cubes and tomato.
7. Cut fish into serving pieces and stir into curry. When fish is covered with sauce, cover pot and simmer for 10-15 minutes or until the red chili powder floats to the top. Fish should then flake easily. Simmering time will depend on thickness of fillets and whether fish were fresh or frozen.
8. Garnish with chopped coriander and sprinkle with lemon juice just before serving.

NOTE: In place of curry powder you can use 1 t. turmeric, ½ t. cumin, and ½ t. crushed coriander.

Tafolu Prawn Salad (Fiji)

Breadfruit
Coconut cream
Corn flour
Onion
Lemon juice or lime juice
Celery or cucumber prawns
Salt
Chili

staples

64

1. Bake a breadfruit in the oven or in the ashes of an open fire, puncturing first with a skewer.
2. Prepare four cups coconut cream.
3. Peel the baked breadfruit.
4. Place the flesh in a large bowl and pound until smooth.
5. Work in the coconut cream until the mixture is a pastry-like consistency. Cut into cubes and roll in balls.
6. Place the rest of the coconut cream in a saucepan with two teaspoons of corn flour for each cup of cream.
7. Bring to boiling point, stirring all the time until thick. Simmer but not boil.
8. Season the thickened cream with one tablespoon of finely chopped onion, one third cup lemon or lime juice, ¾ cup diced celery or cucumber, 1 cup cooked prawns, salt and chili to taste.
9. Combine the prawn cream with the breadfruit.
10. Refrigerate for several hours before serving.
11. Garnish with parsley and lemon slices.
12. Serves 6.

Raw Fish (South Pacific)

1. Using clean fillets of fish remove all bones and skin and cut into ¼ inch pieces.
2. Place in a bowl (not enamel) and add lemon or lime juice to cover.
3. Leave in the marinade 2 hours in a cool place.
4. Grate 1 medium size coconut.
5. Cut 1 lemon into wedges, 1 small onion into slices and chop 1 chili.
6. Combine grated coconut with these ingredients and season with 1 t salt.
7. Add 1 cup water, stir well with hands, squeeze out the cream and strain.
8. Strain fish and discard juice.
9. Pour the flavored coconut cream over the fish, garnish with grated carrot, tomato and lemon slices.
10. Serve in a bowl.

PORK

Baked Stuffed Pawpaw
1 green pawpaw (flesh just turning yellow, but firm)

FILLING:
1 cup finely chopped pork
1 ripe banana, sliced
1 third cup green onions, chopped
1 T. sultanas (optional)
1 third cup scraped coconut (optional)
½ to 1 t. curry powder
1 T. flour

...abus

Part 3: Recipes Using Local Ingredients

¾ pint coconut milk
Salt, pepper to taste
Soy sauce, Gravox, or Vegemite to color (optional)

1. Scrape seeds out of pawpaw.
2. Cut a small slice off the bottom so it will sit flat with the hollow side up. (Don't peel)
3. Heat sufficient oil to cover the bottom of baking pan or frying pan.
4. Cook cut side down till edges are browned (10-15 minutes).
5. Turn and cook other side till tender.

FILLING:

1. Heat oil in frying pan or wok.
2. Stir in pork, onion, banana, curry, flour and fry until pork is cooked.
3. Add coconut and coconut milk and sultanas.
4. Simmer for 15 minutes.
5. Add sufficient soy sauce to make a good color. Add salt and pepper.
6. Place cooked pawpaw on a plate and spoon filling into the hollow.
7. Top with a little scraped coconut.

KUMU

OTA FERN Ota Seisei (Fiji)

1. Choose the tips of the ota fern; the stems should be crisp but not hard.
2. Boil the water.
3. Add the ota fern, make sure that it is completely covered to prevent discoloration.
4. Leave in the boiling water for 2-4 minutes.
5. Drain off the boiling water and put otas into cold water.
6. Split with a lemon spike, pin or knife into fine pieces.
7. Add lemon juice and salt just before serving otherwise the color will change.

VARIATIONS:

1. If the pieces are short, serve mixed with kora (page 99).
2. Can be served with miti (page 99).
3. Can be served with lemon juice and shellfish.

TARO LEAVES

Dalo Leaves in Lolo (Fiji)

Very young taro leaves
Pinch of bicarbonate of soda

kumu..

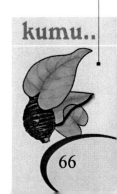

66

Salt to taste
1 onion, finely chopped
Coconut cream

1. Boil the taro leaves until tender with soda and salt and onion.
2. When cooked, strain well.
3. Cover the leaves with coconut cream.
4. Heat again and serve.

Palusami (Samoa)

12 coconuts
120 taro leaves
2 onions, thinly sliced
1 lemon, thinly sliced
Salt and pepper
Breadfruit leaves for wrapping

1. Prepare thick coconut cream.
2. Add onion slices, lemon slices, salt and pepper to the coconut cream and stir for 5 minutes.
3. Take about 6 taro leaves, make them into a cup shape and pour in a cup of the coconut cream mixture. Fold over to stop the coconut cream coming out.
4. Place on a breadfruit leaf and tie the tops.
5. Repeat the process until all the taro leaves are used up.
6. Bake in a hot oven for ½ an hour or steam for about 1 and a ½ hours.

Taro Leaves in Bamboo (Fiji)

Taro leaves, young
Green bamboo, about 2 and a ½ feet long with one end sealed

1. Roll young taro leaves into balls about the size of Brussels sprouts.
2. Place into the green bamboo.
3. Place the bamboo on hot coals and steam 1 and a ½ to 2 hours.

Taveuni Rourou (Fiji)

Young taro leaves (preferably with white stalks)
1 small onion, chopped
A few prawns or fish cutlets
¼ cup grated cheese
Salt and pepper to taste
Chilies (optional)
3 or 4 coconuts

..kumu

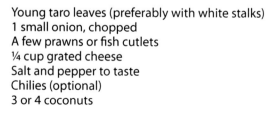
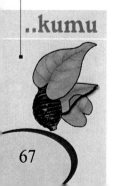

67

1. Grate the coconuts and squeeze out the cream without adding water. Make up one cup.
2. Add salt and pepper to taste and chilies. Put the coconut cream mixture aside.
3. Cut the prawns in halves or chop very finely.
4. Layer the taro leaves, putting the big ones at the bottom, with 4 or 5 small young ones on top. You will be making several bundles of leaves.
5. On top of the layered taro leaves, place 4 halves of the prawns, 2 t. of the grated cheese, a few chopped onions and lastly 2 T. of the coconut cream.
6. Wrap the bundle carefully and fasten it with a toothpick or string. Don't turn the bundle upside down.
7. Repeat with the remaining leaves and stuffing. Six rolls would be sufficient.
8. Add water to the remaining coconut cream and pour over the bundles of food.
9. Cover and cook gently at a medium heat.
10. Serve hot or cold.

STAPLE BANANAS

Baked Tomatoes with Bananas

2 large tomatoes cut in halves
3 bananas
1 t. salt
2 oz. grated cheese
Margarine

1. Put tomatoes in a greased shallow dish.
2. Arrange sliced bananas on top.
3. Brush with melted margarine.
4. Sprinkle with salt and cheese.
5. Bake at 350 F for 20-30 minutes.

Banana Chips (Thailand)

Firm ripe bananas
Lime water
Fat for frying
Sugar
Water

1. Peel ripe bananas still firm and fresh from the tree.
2. Slice as thin as possible, like potato chips.
3. Soak in lime water for 15 or 20 minutes.
4. Drain and fry till brown and crisp in deep fat.

Part 3: Recipes Using Local Ingredients

staples

68

5. In a clean empty pan dissolve granulated sugar in a little water. 6. Add the fried banana chips and stir until they are well coated with the sugar.

Banana Stew

2 lb. beef
2 t. salt
1 t. freshly ground black pepper
3 T. oil
1 cup chopped onions
¾ cup water
One and a ½ cups diced green or cooking bananas

1. Cut the meat in 1-inch cubes; season with the salt and pepper.
2. Heat the oil in a casserole or Dutch oven; brown the meat and onions in it.
3. Add the water; cover and cook over low heat 1 hour or until tender. 4. Add the bananas.
5. Cook 10 minutes or until tender.
6. Serves 4-6.

Fresh Banana Porridge: (Especially for Children)

1 ripe mashed banana
1 T. grated tapioca, taro, kaukau or kumala
1 t. sugar
1 cup milk

1. Mix grated root vegetable with a little milk.
2. Heat rest of milk. Stir in the grated root. Stir over heat until the mixture boils. Boil for a few minutes.
3. Add mashed banana.
4. Serve with milk.

Fried Bananas - I (Thailand)

2 cups boiled taro
3 cups grated coconut
1 cup coconut milk
1 and ¼ cup flour
2 t. sugar
1 and ¼ t. salt
Ripe bananas
Frying fat

staples

69

1. Mash the taro well.
2. Add grated coconut, coconut milk, sugar, flour, and salt.
3. Peel the bananas and slice them.
4. Coat the banana with the above mixture.
5. Fry in hot fat until brown.

ALTERNATIVES:

1. Use sweet potatoes and taro sliced raw as well as the bananas.
2. Use a richer batter:
   ½ cup rice flour (or ¼ cup flour plus ¼ cup cornflour)
   ¼ cup water
   2 T. oil
   2 eggs
   salt
Blend flour, water, oil and salt. Add egg yolks and mix well.
Beat egg whites to a stiff froth and mix lightly with the batter.

Fried Bananas - II (Thailand)

Two third cups each of wheat flour and rice flour (cornflour)
Two third cup palm sugar (brown or natural sugar)
½ cup coconut cream
Small sweet bananas
Fat for frying

1. Blend together the flours, sugar and coconut milk.
2. Let stand for three hours.
3. Peel bananas; press gently with two fingers to break them a little, then dip into the batter.
4. Fry until brown in deep hot fat.

Fried Plantain Cubes (West Africa)

2 mediums sized firm ripe plantains
½ t. ground ginger
¼ t. ground hot red pepper
1 t. salt
1 cup peanut oil

1. Peel the plantains and cut them in half lengthwise.
2. Scoop out the seeds by running the tip of a teaspoon down the center of each half, then cut the plantain into ½ inch cubes.
3. Mix the ginger, red pepper and salt in a bowl, drop the plantain in, and turn the cubes about with a spoon until they are evenly coated with the seasonings.

Part 3: Recipes Using Local Ingredients

staples

70

4. In a heavy 10 to 12 inch skillet, heat the oil over moderate heat until a light haze forms above it.

5. Fry the plantain in the hot oil in two or three batches, turning the cubes gently with a slotted spoon or spatula for 5 to 8 minutes, or until they are browned on all sides.

6. As they brown transfer the cubes to paper towels to drain them.

Green Banana Curry (South Pacific)

2 tablespoons curry powder
1 clove garlic, chopped
1 chili, chopped, sliced or whole
1 small onion, thinly sliced
8 green bananas
Salt
3 Tablespoons oil

1. Peel green bananas and slice.
2. Sprinkle with salt and mix thoroughly.
3. Heat oil in pan, add garlic and onion and chili.
4. Sauté lightly until golden, add curry powder and stir.
5. Add sliced banana and stir-fry at a low heat.
6. Add a little water if necessary.

Serve with grated coconut or chopped nuts.

Spiced Bananas

4 green tipped eating bananas
2 cups sugar
¾ cup vinegar
4 cup lemon juice
2 T. butter
2 sticks cinnamon 1 and a ½ t. whole cloves
1 t. chopped fresh ginger
2 t. salt
4 t. each nutmeg, mace

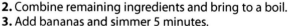

staples

1. Peel banana and cut into 1 inch slices.
2. Combine remaining ingredients and bring to a boil.
3. Add bananas and simmer 5 minutes.
4. Remove bananas from syrup before serving hot or cold with meat.

NOTE: Any left over syrup can be used in cooking ham or pork chops, if you have any.

Stuffed Green Bananas (South Pacific)

6 green bananas
4 oz. raw minced meat
1 chopped onion
1 egg, beaten
Salt and pepper

1. Slice the bananas lengthwise into halves. (Don't peel)
2. Scoop out the flesh with a spoon leaving the fruit boat shaped.
3. Grate the banana flesh.
4. Mix into this, the mince, chopped onion, salt and pepper, and last of all the egg to bind the mixture.
5. Put this filling back into the banana skin and remaining flesh and put the halves together again.
6. Tie with string and steam 25 minutes or bake for approximately 45 minutes. Serve with gravy or with a sauce made from cooked tomatoes.

BREAD AND ALTERNATIVES

Bread-Making (Hints for Beginners)

1. Make sure that everything is at room temperature.
2. Always stir and knead bread in the same direction. This helps to develop the structure of the bread properly.
3. I always knead my bread hard for 10 minutes at least. This means really pounding it. It is hard to over knead bread when doing it by hand.
4. When adding the first lot of flour beat the batter until it is smooth.
5. I have found that when using Canadian recipes I use more flour than it says. This could be because Australian flour is lower in gluten.
6. I have found that to keep the loaves from sticking to the pan I have to grease and then flour the pan.
7. When letting the dough rise I cover it with a piece of plastic and then a tea towel. This prevents a tough crust from forming on the dough.
8. When baking the bread I usually start it at a high temperature and then lower it to finish baking.
9. Yeast - I have found the best results using Fleischmann's in the tins. I have seen it in quite a few places in the country.

Basic White Bread (A recipe especially for tropical baking)

2 levels T. dried yeast or 1 oz. (25 g) fresh yeast
½ cup lukewarm water
1 cup boiling water
1 cup milk

Part 3: Recipes Using Local Ingredients

bread..

72

2 T. butter
2 T. sugar
2 t. salt
6-7 cups flour

1. Rinse a large bowl with hot water to warm it. Add yeast and ½ a cup lukewarm water. Leave to react for 5-10 minutes.
2. In the meantime, mix together the boiling water, milk, butter, sugar and salt. Let cool until it is lukewarm. Add to yeast mixture, stirring well.
3. Measure and sift 3 cups flour. Beat into yeast mixture using a wooden spoon. Thorough beating at this stage reduces the kneading time and results in a more uniform loaf.
4. Measure and sift a further 4 cups of flour. Add this slowly to the mixture, working in the flour with a wooden spoon until it forms a soft dough, which no longer sticks to the side of the bowl. Probably 3 cups or slightly more will be required.
5. Chill for ½ an hour.
6. Place a little of the remaining flour on a board or a clean tabletop and keep the rest handy. Turn dough out onto floured board. Rub a little oil on the hands and form the dough into a rough mound.
7. **To knead:** With fingers and palms resting lightly on the dough, gently draw dough towards you. With "heat" of hand, push quickly away. Give the dough a quarter turn and repeat motion, dusting a little flour when necessary, until the dough is satiny smooth with small bubbles forming on the surface. It will spring back when pressed with the finger. This will take from 5-10 minutes depending on the efficiency of kneading.
8. Place dough in greased bowl and put a little oil on top of dough to prevent a hard crust forming. Cover with a damp cloth and put in a warm place to rise.
9. Leave rise until the dough has doubled in bulk, and a depression made with the finger remains when it is withdrawn. The warmer the day, the more rapidly your dough will rise.
10. Punch dough down and fold sides over. Again leave to rise until it is doubled in bulk. A second rising results in a more tender uniform loaf but can be omitted if you are short of time.
11. Form into 2 large loaves. Dividing in 2 with a knife does this. Roll out to a 6-inch width and 1 inch thickness. Roll up dough very tightly as for a jelly roll, seal edge by moistening with a little water and turn to bottom. Pull the open ends of the rolled dough underneath a tuck in tightly. This results in a smooth uniform loaf.
12. Place in 2 greased 4 inch by 6-inch bread tins, oil top and then let rise until double in bulk.
13. Bake in 375 F oven for 45 to 50 minutes. When done, the bottom will sound hollow when tapped with the finger.

..bread

Mom's Oatmeal Bread (Tested here)

2 cups milk (scalded)
2 cups rolled oats
2 T. sugar
2 t. salt
2 T. shortening
2 T. molasses
2 cup lukewarm water
1 t. sugar
1 pkg. yeast
6-8 cups flour

1. Combine scalded milk, rolled oats, sugar, salt, shortening, and molasses in a large mixing bowl. Cool to lukewarm.
2. Dissolve sugar in water. Sprinkle on yeast. Leave for 10 minutes. Stir into above mixture.
3. Beat in about 4 cups flour, until dough is smooth.
4. Stir in more flour until difficult to work.
5. Turn out on floured surface and knead for 10 minutes.
6. Turn into a large greased bowl and let rise until double.
7. Shape into loaves. Let rise until double.
8. Bake at 400 F for 45-50 minutes.
9. Yield: 2 loaves.

Nearly Fail-Proof buns (A Canadian Recipe that works well)

1 pkg. yeast
½ cup warm water
1 t. sugar
½ cup salad oil
½ cup sugar
2 t. salt
2 cups warm water
Approx. 8 cups flour

1. Dissolve sugar in 2 cups warm water.
2. Sprinkle on yeast and let stand for ten minutes.
3. Combine sugar and oil and beat with a spoon.
4. Add salt, 2 cups warm water, and yeast mixture to oil mixture.
5. Add 4 cups flour and beat until smooth. Work in remaining flour until you can no longer stir it.
6. Turn on floured surface for 10 minutes or until the dough feels smooth and elastic. This is soft dough.
7. Let rise until double, in a greased bowl.
8. Shape into rolls. Let rise until double.

Part 3: Recipes Using Local Ingredients

74

9. Bake at 400 F for about 20 minutes.
10. Yield: 4 dozen.

Oatmeal Bannocks: (For those without an oven and no bread left)

> 6 oz. flour
> 2 t. baking powder
> ¼ t. salt
> 4 oz. margarine or butter
> ½ cup oatmeal
> 2 t. sugar
> ¼ pint milk
> Fat for frying

1. Mix flour with baking powder and salt and rub in fat with fork.
2. Stir in oatmeal and sugar.
3. Make a well in the center and add enough milk to make a soft dough.
4. Break off pieces of dough, roll between floured palms and flatten to make cakes about 2 inches thick.
5. Fry at moderate heat.

VARIATIONS:
1. Substitute flour with 4 oz. mashed potato and 2 oz. flour.
2. Use one egg and ½ the amount of milk.
3. Bake in the oven.

Kaukau Scones

> One and a ½ cups flour
> One and a ½ cups cooked kaukau
> 2 dessert spoons baking powder
> One and a ½ cups butter or margarine
> 1 cup milk
> ¾ t. salt

1. Sift flour, salt, baking powder into a bowl.
2. Rub in margarine with fingers.
3. Combine milk and kaukau.
4. Add to dry ingredients and stir quickly.
5. Knead lightly on floured surface.
6. Cut and place on greased slide.
7. Bake 15-20 minutes at 400 F.

..scone

Quick Banana Scones

> 2 cups flour

Part 3: Recipes Using Local Ingredients

½ t. salt
3 t. baking powder
¼ cup sugar
2 T. butter, melted
½ cup mashed banana
1 egg
2 T. milk

1. Sift flour with other dry ingredients.
2. Combine banana, butter, egg and milk by beating.
3. Make a hollow in the dry ingredients and pour in the liquid ingredients.
4. Mix lightly with a fork.
5. Drop from a spoon onto a greased baking sheet.
6. Bake at 400 F for 15 minutes or until done.

VARIATIONS:

1. Kaukau: use cup cooked mashed kaukau, add 2 cup milk and 2 T. sugar plus 1 t. cinnamon and ½ t. nutmeg.
2. Breadfruit: use 2 cup cooked mashed breadfruit; add ½ cup milk and ½ cup raisins to dry ingredients.

Soda Scones: (For those without an oven and no bread left)

2 cups plain flour
½ t. soda
½ t. cream of tartar
¼ t. salt
¾ of a cup sour milk or buttermilk

1. Mix dry ingredients, add milk to make soft dough.
2. Turn onto floured surface, knead lightly into 2 rounds.
3. Roll or pat to ¼ inch thickness.
4. Cut each round into 4 triangles.
5. Bake on hot, lightly greased griddle or fry pan over medium heat until pale brown.
6. Turn and do other side.
7. Serve hot with lots of butter.

NOTE - Can be used later split and toasted.

Pancakes

2 cups flour
1 egg
Powdered milk and two cups of water or two cups fresh milk
Juice of one lime

pancakes

76

1 t. soda

1. Combine flour, powdered milk, soda
2. Beat egg with water and add to dry ingredients.

Banana Pancakes: I

1 mashed ripe banana
12 T. flour
2 eggs
3 T. sugar
Oil

1. Mix the bananas, flour, eggs and sugar together and beat slightly.
2. Drop 1 T. of the mixture into a frying pan with hot oil. Fry on both sides until crisp and brown.
3. Serve with cinnamon and sugar.

Banana Pancakes: II

1 and one third cups plain flour
3 t. baking powder
½ t. salt
½ t. sugar
Few grains black pepper
1 egg
1 cup milk
3 T. oil or butter
¼ t. vanilla
¾ cup mashed banana

1. Mix dry ingredients and pepper.
2. Beat egg, add milk.
3. Make a well in the dry ingredients, add egg-milk mixture, oil and vanilla.
4. Stir until just mixed.
5. Add banana.
6. Cook a little more slowly than ordinary pancakes.

Sweet Breakfast Fritters

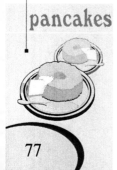

pancakes

1 cup mashed cooked kaukau
2 ripe bananas mashed
1 T. golden syrup or honey
1 t. cinnamon

1. Mix all together and drop into hot oil.
2. Fry both sides.

Part 3: Recipes Using Local Ingredients

CHIPS

Chips

Delicious chips can be made from many starch roots and fruits which are available in the Tropics. The chips should be fried in very hot flavorless salad oil, in a heavy deep saucepan. After cooking, chips should be lifted out and put in a strainer to remove surplus oil and then placed on absorbent paper. Alternatively use a frying basket. The thick type of chips should be kept hot and served as soon as possible. Thin chips may be cooked and stored in a sealed container for future use. If they go soggy, reheat them in a low oven.

Thick Chips

Thick chips may be made from cooked taro, breadfruit, tapioca or kaukau. Bake, boil or steam any of the preceding vegetables until soft, but still firm. Cut into pieces about 1-12 inches long and 4 inch thick. Fry in hot oil until crisp and brown. Dust with salt and pepper.

Thin Chips

Thin chips may be made from kaukau, green bananas and cooking bananas. Green bananas may be peeled like a potato using a paring knife. Rub a little oil on the hand to prevent staining.

Cut very thin slices with a potato peeler or a very sharp knife. Put slices to soak in a bowl of water for 2 hours to draw out excess starch. Take out and dry on a cloth. Fry in hot oil until crisp and brown. Dust with salt and pepper just before serving. Do not add salt ahead of time as chips are inclined to go soft.

Cassava Drops

Grate raw tapioca on a fine grater and season with salt and pepper. Form into small round balls by gently rolling in the hands. Drop into hot oil and fry until golden brown. Just before serving they may be sprinkled with additional salt or a little curry powder, ground cumin, basil or any other desired spices or herbs.

KAUKAU

Kaukau and Banana Casserole

> 4 kaukau
> One and a ½ t. salt
> 4 T. butter
> 4 bananas

chips..

78

¾ cup brown sugar
2 cups orange juice

1. Cook the unpeeled kaukau in boiling water until tender but firm.
2. Drain, peel and slice 4 inch thick.
3. In a buttered casserole, arrange alternate layers of the kaukau sprinkled with salt and dotted with butter, and the banana sprinkled with brown sugar. Start with the kaukau and end with the banana layer dotted with butter.
4. Add the orange juice.
5. Bake in a 350 F oven for 30 minutes or until browned on top.
6. Serves 6-8.

Kaukau and Pineapple Casserole

Kaukau
Grated coconut
Butter
Sliced pineapple

1. Boil the unpeeled kaukau until tender.
2. Drain, peel and slice kaukau 2 inches thick.
3. Grease baking dish and sprinkle with grated coconut.
4. Dot with small pieces of butter.
5. Arrange layer of pineapple on bottom of the baking dish.
6. Top with a layer of kaukau.
7. Repeat.
8. Bake in a hot oven for 2 hour.

Kaukau Puff

4 kaukau (depending on their size)
1 t. salt
4 T. sugar
2 cups coconut cream
2 T. butter
2 cup grated coconut

1. Boil the unpeeled kaukau until tender.
2. Drain, peel and mash very smooth.
3. Beat in the salt, sugar and coconut cream.
4. Turn into a buttered 9-inch pie plate.
5. Bake in a 400 F degree oven for 20 minutes or until delicately browned.
6. Melt the butter in a skillet; lightly brown the coconut in it.
7. Sprinkle on top of the kaukau puff.
8. Serve hot or cold.

Part 3: Recipes Using Local Ingredients

..chips

Lemon-Buttered Kaukau

12 medium kaukau
½ cup melted butter or margarine
¼ cup lemon juice or lime juice
2 t. grated lemon or lime rind
½ t. pepper
½ cup brown sugar, packed.

1. Scrub kaukau well. Put in a large pot and cover with boiling water. Boil until tender. Cool until they can be handled.
2. Peel kaukau and cut in half lengthwise.
3. Lay kaukau slices in two 13 by 9 and a ½ inch baking dishes in a single layer if possible.
4. Heat oven to 450 F.
5. Combine butter, lemon juice, lemon rind and pepper.
6. Pour half of this mixture over the potatoes in each baking dish.
7. Heat 10 minutes or until hot, basting several times.
8. Turn on broiler.
9. Baste again and sprinkle with sugar.
10. Broil 2 or 3 minutes or just until sugar begins to bubble.
11. Serve hot.

Stewed Sweet Potatoes (Southern Africa)

¼ cup brown sugar
1 T. flour
1 t. salt
2 pounds kaukau peeled and sliced into 2-inch-rounds
3 T. butter, cut into 4 inch bits
3 one-inch pieces of stick cinnamon
¼ cup water

1. Combine the sugar, flour and salt in a small bowl and stir them together.
2. Place about one third of the kaukau in a heavy saucepan, overlapping the slices to cover the bottom of the pan completely.
3. Sprinkle the kaukau with about one third of the sugar mixture and dot the top with 1 T. of the butter bits.
4. Cover the first layer with another third of the kaukau, another third of the sugar mixture and 1 T. of the butter. Then arrange the remaining kaukau on top and sprinkle them with the rest of the sugar and butter bits.
5. Tuck the cinnamon under the top layer of kaukau and pour the water down the side of the pot.
6. Bring to a boil over high heat, cover tightly, and reduce the heat to low. Slide the pot back and forth occasionally to prevent the bottom layer from scorching and simmer the kaukau for 45

chips..

minutes or until they are soft but still intact.

7. With a slotted spoon, transfer the potatoes to a heated bowl and moisten them with about a ½ cup of the cooking liquid.

8. Serve at once.

RICE

Yellow Coconut Rice (Indonesia)

1. Measure 1 cup of coconut cream for every cup of raw rice.

2. Wash rice and place in a saucepan with ½ tsp. of turmeric.

3. Cover with water and boil until the rice is half cooked. (The centre is still hard when bitten.)

4. While the rice is boiling, bring the coconut milk just to a boil with 1 bay leaf, ½ tsp. loas (optional), 1 tsp. turmeric and ½ tsp. salt.

5. Strain the half-cooked rice and transfer to the coconut milk mixture. Allow standing away from the fire for a minute.

6. Continue cooking slowly until the liquid is absorbed. (Use an asbestos pad on gas elements.)

Coconut Rice (Burma)

> 5 cups rice
> 1 T. vegetable oil
> One-third t. salt
> 2 coconuts
> 1 t. sugar
> 2 onions

1. Grate the coconuts, add ½ cup hot water and squeeze through a thin sieve.

2. Repeat till all the milk is extracted.

3. Wash rice thoroughly.

4. Pour rice into a pot.

5. Add to the rice: oil, sugar, salt and onions. Stir until well mixed.

6. Cover with coconut milk and cook until the milk is evaporated and the rice is tender.

TARO

Baseisei (Fiji)

> Taro stalks
> Lemon juice
> Salt

1. Peel off the thin layer of skin on the taro stalks and tie the stalks

Part 3: Recipes Using Local Ingredients

into bundles.
2. Put the bundles into boiling water and boil for 8-10 minutes with the lid on the saucepan.
3. When tender put into cold water.
4. Cut off the ends and gently scrape the stalks to remove any discolored part and extra skin.
5. Split into thin pieces with a lemon spike, needle, pin or knife.
6. Remove from the water and drain well.
7. Serve with lemon juice and salt.

VARIATION:

1. Serve with miti (page 99).
2. Add spring onion.

YAMS

Nyoma (Ghana)

6 medium-sized yams
Small piece salt beef
¾ lb. meat
¼ lb. lard
1 t. salt
1 t. pepper

1. Peel yams wash and cut them into ½ inch pieces.
2. Cook slowly in water.
3. Cut the meat into small pieces and cook with the yam.
4. When the yam and meat are cooked add lard, salt and pepper.
5. Mix well and serve hot.

Ota (Ghana)

5 lb. yam
¼ lb. dripping or butter
1 t. salt
5 eggs
2 tomatoes
4 onions
½ t. ground pepper

1. Peel, wash and cut yam into small pieces. Boil in salted water until soft.
2. Meanwhile, finely chop tomatoes and onions and fry in some of the dripping or butter until soft.

Part 3: Recipes Using Local Ingredients

chips..

82

3. When the yams are tender, drain and mash with the rest of the dripping or butter and add the vegetables and pepper.
4. Serve hot with hard boiled eggs.

Yam Soup

> 1 lb. yams
> 2 cup sliced onions
> 3 cups water
> 3 T. butter
> 3 cups milk
> One and a ½ t. salt
> 4 t. pepper

1. Cook the yams and onions in the water for 20 minutes.
2. Force the undrained mixture through a sieve.
3. Return to the saucepan and stir in the butter, milk, salt and pepper.
4. Heat and serve.
5. Serves 4-6.

ALTERNATIVE: Use coconut milk.

VEGETABLES

BANANA BLOSSOM

Banana Blossom: (South Pacific)

> 2 small banana blossoms
> 1 cup shelled shrimps plus 2 cups of the juice they were boiled in
> 4 cloves chopped garlic
> 1 onion cut in slices
> Oil for frying
> Vinegar, salt and pepper to taste

..chips

1. Remove the tough covering of the blossom. Slice thin (crosswise).
2. Squeeze it with salt and rinse. Set aside.
3. Mix the shrimps, sliced onions, and vinegar.
4. Sauté the garlic and add the shrimp mixture.
5. Add the juice or water and continue cooking. Add the blossom.
6. Turn over constantly until tender. Season with salt.

BEANS

Beans in Coconut (South India)

One and a ½ pounds French beans or long green beans
1 red chili
1 medium onion
2-4 cloves garlic
2 T. oil, grease or fat
½ a cup of finely grated coconut
Salt to taste

1. Slice the beans finely.
2. Heat oil and put in chopped onion, chili and garlic. Brown slightly.
3. Add the beans. Fry for a few minutes. Add salt.
4. Cover and steam slowly until the beans are tender.
5. Add the coconut.
6. If necessary, add a little water while steaming, but all the water must be absorbed before adding the coconut.

EGGPLANT

Eggplant Baked in Coconut Cream (South Pacific)

4 to 6 eggplants
2 coconuts for cream
1 onion, sliced
Salt to taste
1 chili, chopped

1. Peel and slice the eggplant. Soak in a bowl of salted water for 15 to 20 minutes to remove any discoloration.
2. Place the eggplant slices in a baking dish.
3. Cover the eggplant with the onion slices.
4. Add the salt and chili.
5. Squeeze the coconut cream over the eggplant and onions.
6. Cover the dish and bake slowly in a moderate oven.

VARIATION: Steam

Eggplant in Batter

2 eggplants
½ a small onion
2 cloves garlic
1 and a ½ tsp. curry powder
½ cup flour

chips..

84

3 tsp. salt
7 T. water
Fat for frying

1. Slice eggplants and soak in a bowl of salted water while preparing the batter.
2. Chop onions, garlic and chilies.
3. Mix all the ingredients except the fat and eggplant slices into a smooth batter.
4. Dip the pieces of eggplant into the batter.
5. Fry until brown.

PAWPAW

Sajur Pepaja (Indonesia)

1 half-ripe pawpaw
1 small onion
½ t. nutmeg
Salt
2 T. butter
1 T. flour
¼ t. pepper
Water or coconut milk to cover

1. Peel pawpaw and cut into one and a ½ by ¼ pieces; boil until tender; drain.
2. Slice onions finely and stir-fry in oil until softened; add the flour gradually stirring constantly.
3. Then add water or coconut milk; still stirring; next pepper, nutmeg and salt.
4. When the liquid is thick add the pawpaw and beat.

ALTERNATIVE: Substitute marrow or choko.

Steamed Papaya (East Africa)

One and a ½ lbs. under-ripe pawpaw, peeled, seeded and cut into one and a ½ inch cubes
4 T. butter
1/8 t. ground nutmeg
½ t. salt

1. Spread the pawpaw cubes on the rack of a steamer or in a bowl above boiling water in a pot.
2. Cover the pan tightly and steam over moderate heat for 15 to 20 minutes.
3. When the pawpaw is tender and somewhat translucent, transfer it to sieve or colander to drain.

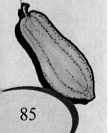

Part 3: Recipes Using Local Ingredients

4. Melt the butter in a heavy pan over moderate heat.

5. Drop in the pawpaw and season it with the nutmeg and salt.

6. Toss the pawpaw gently with a spoon until it is evenly coated with the butter.

PUMPKIN

Curried Pumpkin Chips

8 oz. fresh pumpkin
Cooking oil
1 T. curry powder
2 t. salt
One-eighth t. garlic powder

1. Slice pumpkin one sixteenth inch thick. (two cups)

2. Soak in ice water for 1 hour.

3. Drain and pat dry.

4. Fry in hot oil until browned. (about 2 minutes)

5. Drain on paper towels.

6. Combine curry, salt and garlic powder.

7. Sprinkle over chips.

Pumpkin with Coconut Milk (Philippines)

1 small pumpkin, cubed
3 cloves garlic, crushed
1 cup small prawns, peeled
1 cup prawn juice from the heads of the prawns salt and pepper
1 cup coconut milk

1. Brown garlic in fat.

2. Add the prawns; then the prawn juice, and simmer for 10 minutes, stirring constantly.

3. Add pumpkin and cook until almost done.

4. Season with salt and pepper.

5. Just before removing from the heat, add coconut milk and continue simmering for a few minutes, stirring well.

MIXED VEGETABLES

Vegetables in Batter

2 cup flour
2 cup cornflour salt

chips..

1 t. baking powder
1 egg, beaten
Cold water
Thinly sliced vegetables

1. Combine dry ingredients. You may add more flour but make sure you always have equal parts of flour and cornflour.
2. Add the egg and water to make a soupy mixture.
3. Dip in the vegetables and fry in hot fat. The flour mixture will puff up and brown.
4. Drain before serving.

Vegetable Curry

1 oz. cooking oil or fat
1 chopped onion
1 clove chopped garlic
2 chopped chilies
1 T. curry powder
2 cups vegetables (any kind)
2 t. salt
1 cup water or coconut cream

1. Heat the oil or fat and fry the onion, chilies and garlic.
2. When brown, add the curry powder and stir well, add the vegetables and salt.
3. Cook for a little while and then add water or coconut cream and cook until tender.

SWEETS

CAKES

Banana Cake (Tested)

½ cup shortening
One and a ½ cup sugar
2 eggs
Two third cup sour milk
1 cup mashed bananas
Cup nuts (optional)
2 cups flour
1 t. soda
1 t. baking powder
1 t. Salt
1 t. vanilla

sweets

87

1. Use conventional cake method of mixing.
2. Cream shortening, add sugar and continue creaming.
3. Add beaten whole eggs and vanilla and stir.
4. Sift dry ingredients together and add alternately with milk to the creamed mixture.
5. Stir in bananas and nuts.
6. Place mixture into two round 8-inch or 1 rectangular baking dish.
7. Bake at 350 F for 35 minutes or till done.

Banana Loaf

2 cup butter
1 cup sugar
2 eggs well beaten
2 large ripe bananas-well beaten
2 T. milk
2 cups self-raising flour
½ t. salt

1. Cream butter and sugar.
2. Mix in the order given.
3. Bake in a greased loaf pan in a slow oven (300 F) for 1 hour.

Cassava Cake (Philippines)

3-4 cups grated tapioca
1 cup grated coconut
¼ cup of sugar to each cup of grated tapioca
Coconut milk

1. Toss tapioca and coconut together.
2. Place in a baking tray.
3. Pour coconut milk over to make a slightly soupy mixture.
4. Bake in a moderate oven until golden brown on top.

Cassava Suman (Philippines)

1 cup grated tapioca
2 cup grated and chopped coconut
¾ cup sugar
Banana leaves

1. Mix all the ingredients and wrap mixture in 2 layers of wilted banana leaves to size desired.
2. Tie the ends with string.
3. Boil in water until done.

sweets

Cassava Sweet Cake

Large tapioca root
Sugar to taste
2 eggs
Coconut milk
Cinnamon (optional)

1. Grate tapioca and add sugar and eggs.
2. Squeeze in coconut milk, preferably from a young coconut.
3. Spoon into a glass baking dish and sprinkle with cinnamon.

Pumpkin Cake

½ cup margarine or butter
One and a ½ cups brown sugar
2 and a ½ cups self-raising flour
½ t. salt
¼ t. each - nutmeg, ginger, cinnamon
3 eggs
1-cup cold mashed pumpkin
Milk, if necessary

1. Cream butter and sugar.
2. Add eggs and beat well.
3. Add spices, then pumpkin. Mix.
4. Add sifted flour and salt.
5. Mix until smooth.
6. Put mixture into greased and lined 9 by 13 cake pan.
7. Bake at 350 F for 35 minutes.

Very good served with custard sauce.

JAMS
Banana Jam

6 large bananas
1 cup lemon juice
2 t. grated lemon rind
1 cup water sugar
2 t. chopped ginger

1. Squeeze the juice of the lemons and grate rinds.
2. Add the water and chopped ginger.
3. Slice the bananas into this measure.
4. Bring to a boil and add an equal amount of sugar.
5. Boil until it is a good red colour. Stir frequently.
6. Pour into hot clean jars and cover.

Part 3: Recipes Using Local Ingredients

sweets

89

Part 3: Recipes Using Local Ingredients

Coconut Papaya Jam

3 cups crushed fresh papaya
1 cup freshly grated coconut
7 and a ½ cups sugar
¼ cup lemon juice

1. Combine papaya with coconut, sugar, and lemon juice.
2. Cook the mixture over high heat until it comes to a full rolling boil.
3. Boil until thick, stirring regularly.
4. Cool the jam for 5 to 10 minutes, stirring constantly to keep the fruit from separating.
5. Pour into hot sterilized jars and seal with paraffin.

NOTE: If commercial pectin is available, step 3 should read: Remove mixture from heat and add 2 bottle of commercial pectin, stirring vigorously. This will give you a thicker jam.

Passion-fruit Jam

12 passion fruits
3 cups cold water
Juice of 2 lemons
1 and ¼ pounds of sugar

1. Scoop out pulp from passion-fruit, put ½ the shells into a bowl, pour over 2 and a ½ cups of water and leave overnight.
2. Next day bring to boil, then cook gently for about 35 minutes or until the inside of the shells are tender.
3. Save the water.
4. Scoop out inside pulp and chop. Discard skin.
5. Put pulp, fruit and seeds into a pot with the reserved water. Add the other ½ cup of water and bring to the boil.
6. Add lemon juice and warmed sugar.
7. Stir until sugar has dissolved and boil rapidly until the jam sets.
8. Cool for a few minutes and then put into warm sterilized jars and seal.

Pawpaw Butter

1 cup sieved cooked pawpaw
1 piece ginger cooked with pawpaw
2 cups sugar
2 t. cinnamon
1/8 t. cloves
4 T. lemon juice
1 t. salt

sweets

90

1. Boil all together till a little will jell when cooled.

Pawpaw Marmalade

> 5-6 medium sized pawpaw, chopped into small pieces
> 2-3 cups sugar (to taste)
> Juice of 2-3 large lemons or 3-4 muli
> Grated rind of 2-3 large lemons or 3-4 muli
> 3-4 t. of chopped fresh ginger or to taste

1. Mix chopped pawpaw with sugar, leave overnight.
2. Transfer fruit, sugar and accumulated juices to a large pot.
3. Add remaining ingredients and cook over low heat for about 1 hour until a thermometer register 220 F or until the juices are thickened.
4. Pour into hot, sterilized jars. Cover straight away.
5. Makes 2-3 fairly big jars.

VARIATION: Use chopped or thinly sliced limes or muli. Use chopped pineapple.

Pineapple and Papaya Jam

Reduce ripe papaya to a fine pulp and to each cup add 1 cup of chopped pineapple and ¾ cup of sugar.

Boil until thick.

Pack in sterilized jars.

NOTE: The juice of one lime makes this tastier. Add while boiling.

Tomato-Lemon/Lime Jam

> 5 lbs. firm tomatoes, peeled
> 5 lbs. sugar
> 3 unpeeled lemons or limes, thinly sliced
> 1 T. grated fresh ginger

1. Chop tomatoes coarsely and place in a heavy saucepan in alternate layers with sugar and lemon or lime slices.
2. Add ginger and stirring frequently simmer slowly over medium-low heat until jam is thick, about 40-50 minutes.
3. Pour into 4 or 5 hot sterilized jars, seal and store.

sweets

Part 3: Recipes Using Local Ingredients

Watermelon Rind Honey

In this recipe you wash and peel off the dark green outer rind and the red meat and use the pale green inner rind.

> 6 cups peeled watermelon rind
> 1 unpeeled lemon or lime, sliced paper-thin
> ¼ t. salt
> 6 cups sugar
> 2 t. grated fresh ginger
> Two 1 inch cinnamon sticks
> ½ t. whole cloves

1. Put rind through food grinder, using coarse blade or chop very finely.
2. Then cook slowly in a heavy saucepan until the rind is transparent, about 25 minutes, stirring a few times.
3. Add lemon, salt, sugar and ginger and stir until sugar partly dissolves.
4. Add cinnamon and cloves tied in cheesecloth.
5. Cook over low heat, stirring often, until the mixture is somewhat thick, about 1 hour.
6. Remove spices and fill 8 hot sterilized jars within an inch of the top.
7. Seal and store.

PIES

Banana Pie

> Basic short crust pastry
> 4 cups sliced, green tipped bananas
> Juice of 1 lemon (or 2 limes) plus pineapple juice to make a ¼ cup
> ½ cup sugar
> 1 t. cinnamon
> 2 t. flour
> 2 t. butter

1. Soak bananas in juice for 20-30 minutes.
2. Cover bottom of pie pan with pastry.
3. Place bananas in pie pan. (without the marinade)
4. Blend together: sugar, cinnamon, and flour and sprinkle over bananas.
5. Add 3 T. of the juice and dot with the butter.
6. Cover with top crust, which has slits cut in it.
7. Seal and bake for 30 minutes or until browned.
8. Serve warm topped with ice cream.

Part 3: Recipes Using Local Ingredients

sweets

Buko Pie

Basic short crust pastry
2 cups young coconut meat cut in squares
1/3 cup cornstarch blended with:
  ½ cup young coconut milk
  ½ cup evaporated milk
  ¾ cup sugar

Combine the ingredients together in a saucepan. Cook slowly until thick. Use for pie filling.

Kaukau Pie

Basic short crust pastry
1 cup cold sieved kaukau
1 and two thirds cup evaporated milk
2 eggs
¾ cup sugar
1 T. lemon juice
Nutmeg

1. Prepare two pie shells ready for the oven.
2. Beat together; milk, eggs, sugar, kaukau, and lemon juice.
3. Place in unbaked pie shell.
4. Sprinkle the top with a little freshly grated nutmeg and sugar.
5. Bake at 450 F for 10 minutes.
6. Reduce heat to 325 F and continue baking for a further 40 to 50 minutes. It will be done when the filling slightly puffs up and a knife inserted in the middle comes out clean.
7. Chill pie thoroughly and serve.
Good served with ice cream or chocolate sauce.

Pawpaw and Banana Pie

1 piecrust
2 T. butter
2 T. flour
1 and ¼ cups scraped pawpaw pulp
dash of vinegar or 2 t. lime juice
¼ t. salt
1-2 T. syrup depending on the ripeness of the pawpaw
½ t. ginger
Nutmeg
3-4 ripe bananas

1. Melt margarine, stir in flour and cook a little until it is bubbly.
2. Stir in pawpaw pulp, boil 2-3 minutes stirring all the time.

sweets

Part 3: Recipes Using Local Ingredients

93

3. Cool and stir in flavourings. (Not nutmeg)
4. Add sliced bananas.
5. When quite cool put into pie shell and sprinkle with nutmeg.

Pineapple Pie Filling

Dice one pineapple and boil until soft with ½ cup sugar. Thicken with 2 T. corn flour mixed to smooth paste with water.

Passionfruit Pie Filling

> 1 cup water
> 2 T. butter
> 2-3 heaped T. custard powder
> 1 cup sugar
> Pulp of 4 large passionfruit

1. Boil together water, sugar and butter.
2. Mix passionfruit and custard powder and add to boiling mixture and stir continuously until thick and bubbling.
3. Cool slightly and add to cold pastry case.

Lemon or Lime Pie Filling

Same as above only substitute juice of 1 lemon or lime for passion fruit.

Pawpaw Pie Filling

1. Dice a ripe but firm pawpaw.
2. Mix in 4 T. sugar, 2 T. sultanas, dash of lemon or orange juice, and 2 T. golden syrup.
3. Turn into a pastry shell and cover with pastry.

Tropical Apple Pie

> Basic short crust
> 6 to 8 slices green mangoes
> Two thirds cup sugar (or to taste)
> 1 T. flour
> 1 t. cinnamon or nutmeg

1. Mix mangoes, sugar, flour and spice together until well blended.
2. Place mixture in unbaked crust.
3. Place top crust on pie and fasten securely at edges.
4. Bake in a hot, 450 F oven for 10 minutes, then reduce the heat to 350 F and continue baking for about 25 to 30 minutes longer until the crust is nicely browned.
You could substitute guavas for the mangoes.

Part 3: Recipes Using Local Ingredients

sweets

94

Crust-less Tropical Fruit Pie

In a square buttered pan, put 8 slices of mangoes or guavas, sprinkle with 1 T. lemon juice. Put the following mixture on top:

> ½ cup brown sugar
> ½ cup flour
> ½ cup butter
> pinch of salt

Rub ingredients together to resemble crumbs. Bake in 350 F oven for 40 minutes. You could substitute pawpaws, pineapples, bananas or any other fruit that may be available in your area.

Tropical Peach Pie

> Short crust
> 1 and ½ cups flour
> ½ cup oil or margarine or butter
> 4 T. cold water
> 2 t. salt

1. Sift flour and salt.
2. Rub in fat.
3. Toss in water using a fork.
4. Form a ball. Let stand 5 minutes in the refrigerator if possible.
5. Divide the dough into two. Roll each half out 1 inch bigger than the pie plate.
6. Fit one into the pan.

Filling:

> 1 small pawpaw
> 2 T. corn flour
> 4 T. sugar
> 2 cups water
> Nutmeg

1. Peel and cube pawpaw.
2. Cook with water until mushy.
3. Mix sugar and cornflour and a little water to make a smoot paste.
4. Stir into hot pawpaw sauce.
5. Cool slightly.
6. Pour sauce into unbaked shell.
7. Sprinkle with nutmeg.
8. Top with second crust and vent.
9. Bake until golden brown.

sweets

Custard Sauce:

>   1 pint milk
>   1 egg
>   2 T. corn flour
>   ½ t. salt
>   1 t. vanilla

1. Mix all ingredients until smooth.
2. Cook, stirring constantly over low heat until thick and smooth.
3. Stir in vanilla and cool.

PUDDINGS

Bananas with Coconut Sauce

>   6 half-ripe bananas
>   1 cup milk
>   1 cup fresh finely grated coconut 4 cup sugar

1. Place the whole unpeeled banana into boiling water and cook carefully until soft. (20-30 minutes).
2. Drain off the water, remove the skins and cut the bananas lengthwise.
3. To make the sauce, heat the grated coconut in the milk. Add the sugar.
4. Pour the sauce over the bananas.

Banana Pudding

>   4 bananas
>   1 and a ½ cups coconut milk
>   4 T. sugar
>   2 T. cornstarch
>   2 cup water
>   1 t. vanilla extract if available
>   2 drops red food coloring if available

1. Peel the bananas and cut in 2-inch lengths.
2. Cook in the coconut milk until very soft.
3. Add sugar and mash smooth.
4. Mix the cornstarch and water and stir into the banana mixture.
5. Cook over low heat, stirring steadily until thickened.
6. Add the vanilla and food coloring.
7. Pour into molds and chill.
8. Serve with coconut cream.

Part 3: Recipes Using Local Ingredients

pudding

96

Ripe Bananas in Coconut Cream

1 coconut
6 bananas

1. Prepare coconut cream.
2. Peel bananas.
3. Place bananas in banana leaf and pour coconut cream over them, wrap them up.
4. Bake in a mumu together with other food.

VARIATION: Bake in an oven or steam.

Haupia - Hawaiian Coconut Pudding

1/3 cup sifted cornstarch
1/3 cup sugar
3 cups coconut milk

1. Mix the cornstarch and sugar in a saucepan.
2. Gradually stir in the coconut milk.
3. Cook over low heat, stirring steadily until thickened.
4. Pour into an 8 inch square buttered pan.
5. Chill until set.
6. Cut into squares and serve.

VARIATION: After you have poured the mixture into the pan, sprinkle the top with ¼ cup of scraped coconut.

Sun-dried Bananas

Very ripe but firm bananas

1. Peel and scrape well. Place in the sun under a wire cover and turn often. In about 4-5 days the fruit will have turned brown. Store in closed tins or jars.
2. If inclined to be hard, sprinkle with sugar and place in warm oven for about 5 hours. The fruit, when ready, should be moist and brown.
3. Serve as a dessert or chop up well and add to fruit cake instead of dates, figs or other imported fruits.

pudding

Do not-try to dry bananas unless the weather is sunny and the air is dry.

Dried Banana Pudding

4 dried bananas
½ pint milk
4 eggs
1 oz. fine sugar

Part 3: Recipes Using Local Ingredients

A squeeze of lemon juice Pinch of salt

1. Cut bananas across in small pieces and stew in the milk for about ½ hour.
2. Beat eggs and sugar and add the stewed bananas and milk.
3. Pour into mold and steam for 45 minutes.
4. Turn out of mold and serve either hot or cold with custard sauce.

Vakalavalava (Fijian)

2 cups grated tapioca
½ cup sugar
1 cup grated coconut
2 mashed bananas

1. Mix the grated tapioca, grated coconut, mashed banana and sugar.
2. Wrap in a softened banana leaf and bake or steam for about 45 minutes.

Vakalolo Sakosako (Fiji)

Taro cooked in the skin
1 cup sugar
2 cups coconut cream

1. Skin and pound the taro until it becomes a dough.
2. Cut into pieces or form into balls.
3. Heat the sugar and coconut cream together until the mixture is brown.
4. Soak the pieces of taro in the mixture.
5. Wrap in leaves for serving or put in a dish.

VARIATIONS:
1. Use tapioca or breadfruit instead of taro.
2. Do not heat the sugar and coconut cream.
3. Vakalolo 'Sivaro Maca'. Use a mixture of taro and tapioca. Use grated coconut instead of coconut cream. Heat the sugar until it melts. Add the grated coconut and heat until it is brown.

pudding

98

MISCELLANEOUS

SAUCES

Part 3: Recipes Using Local Ingredients

Kora (Fiji)

2 coconuts
1 cup boiled seawater or 1 cup water plus 1 T. salt pepper or chilies
2 t. lemon juice
1 t. grated onion

1. Grate one coconut and squeeze out the cream.
2. Mix the grated flesh with water.
3. Put in a jar, cover and leave in a warm place.
4. Stir daily for 1 week.
5. At the end of the fermentation period, the coconut should have a soft, smooth consistency. Strain off the liquid.
6. Squeeze the cream from 1 grated coconut (do not add water). Mix the cream with the fermented coconut flesh. Flavor with pepper or chopped chilies, lemon juice and grated onion.
7. Serve with fish, on biscuits as a cheese-like spread.

NOTE: You must use fresh coconut for kora.

Miti (Fiji)

1 coconut, grated
1 lemon, sliced with skin on
1 or 2 chilies, chopped
2 T. chopped onion
1 t. salt

1. Place grated coconut in a bowl.
2. Add lemon, chilies, onion, and salt.
3. Blend well and leave for 1 or 2 hours.
4. Squeeze out coconut cream using your hands.
5. Strain.

VARIATION: Add 1 cup water to coconut before squeezing. This will make a weaker sauce.

Sambal Goreng Tomat (peppered tomatoes) (Indonesia)

1 and a ½ T. oil
2 cloves garlic
1 medium onion, minced
1 or more crushed dry chili peppers or 1 t. chili powder

6 firm tomatoes, quartered, preferably under-ripe
1 and ½ t. brown sugar
1 t. salt
1 and a ½ t. pepper or to taste
2 cups coconut milk

1. Heat oil in a skillet and add garlic, onion and crushed chili peppers.
2. Sauté lightly for 2 minutes.
3. Add tomatoes, sugar, salt and pepper. Stir and cook 2 or 3 minutes or until tomatoes are quite tender.
4. Add coconut milk and cook uncovered to a thick pulpy consistency.
5. Remove garlic, if you wish, when cooking is complete.

SOUPS

Coconut Soup

2 t. curry powder
One and ½ T. cornstarch
3 cups beef broth
3 cups coconut cream

1. Mix the curry powder and cornstarch with a little broth, then add the remaining broth.
2. Cook over low heat, stirring steadily to the boiling point.
3. Cook over low heat for 10 minutes.
4. Stir in the coconut cream; but do not let it boil.

Serves 6-8.

WINES

Banana Wine

2 pounds peeled bananas
½ lb. banana skins
¼ lb. raisins
1 lemon
1 orange
3 lb. sugar
1 gallon water
yeast and nutrient
1. Use black or spotted bananas.
2. Place bananas and fruit peel into a cloth bag and put the bag, tied up, into a large saucepan or boiler with water.
3. Bring to a boil and simmer for ½ an hour.
4. Pour hot liquor over sugar and fruit juice.

wine...

100

Part 3: Recipes Using Local Ingredients

5. When the bag has cooled squeeze it to extract as much liquor as possible.
6. When all liquor is lukewarm (70 F) add yeast.
7. Leave in a warm place for one week, stirring daily.
8. Then pour into a glass jar and store in a cooler place. (it will be a thick-looking mess like a lot of soapsuds)
9. Keep it well covered and in a couple of months it will have a large sediment at the bottom. Siphon off; then add the chopped raisins.
10. Fit an air lock and siphon off again after 4 months, by then it will have started to clear.
11. Leave for a further six months before sampling.
12. It improves with age.

NOTE:
1. The wine making process may be speeded up in the tropics.
2. Make sure all your equipment is sterilized to prevent the introduction of new bacteria into your wine.

MEASURES: Part 4 – Additional Information
AUSTRALIAN MEASURES

If you use Australian recipes, some measurements are different to those you may be used to in Canada.

TABLESPOON: In Canada a tablespoon is ½ oz, but in Australia it is 1 oz. One Australian tablespoon equals two Canadian tablespoons.

DESSERT SPOON: It is somewhere between a Canadian tablespoon and an Australian tablespoon. Try a heaped Canadian tablespoon.

PINT: An Australian pint is 20 fluid ounces or 2 and ½ cups, not 16 ounces or 2 cups as in the American pint.

Solid measures are often given in ounces. Here is a table comparing these measures with Canadian measures.

½ oz. = 1 tablespoon
2 oz. = ½ cup
4 oz. = 1 cup
16 oz. = 4 cups

measures

South Pacific recipes tend to be written in both Australian and American measures. Often you can use clues to decide which measures have been used if you're not sure. Words such as dessert spoon, castor sugar, cornflour, wholemeal flour, or scones would indicate an Australian recipe. If the solid measures are given in ounces, you could be fairly sure that it is an Australian recipe. But, then just to keep you from being confused, newer recipes are beginning to be written in metric.

To help a little, many supermarkets in PNG sell a handy cone-shaped measuring utensil that has all the different measures written along its sides.

This collection has been written in standard North American measurements which most Canadians are accustomed to.

CASSAVA OR TAPIOCA STARCH

tapioca (cassava)
piece of cotton, flour bag or loosely woven material

1. Peel and grate the cassava root and tie in the bag.
2. Squeeze thoroughly, wash this in a bucket or basin of water.
3. When all the white, milky fluid seems to have been squeezed out of the grated cassava, remove it and let the water stand until the white starch settles.
4. Pour off this water, add more and stir up the starch again before allowing it to settle once more.
5. Do this twice more during the day.
6. Pour off the water and leave the basin in the sun until the starch is thoroughly dry.
7. To make a fine flour, the starch should be rolled and sieved. It will keep for a long time in a jar or tin with a lid on.

USES
1. To thicken puddings, sauces, stews.
2. In any recipe in place of cornflour.
3. For starching clothes.

COFFEE AND TEA

Excellent coffee and tea are grown in PNG. You will probably develop a preference for products from particular areas if there is a choice available in the stores in your town.

You can buy roasted beans or pre-ground coffee and use a percolator or filters. Many CUSO's merely place the ground coffee in a saucepan and boil it until the desired strength is obtained. There is a controversy over whether boiling or water from the tap should be added to the grounds. One CUSO here has developed a method for making coffee ahead of time for a period in the day when you may not have access to electricity.
"I found making coffee in a thermos the answer to lunch breaks without electricity. (Our power in Minj goes off at 0930,

measures

and comes on at 1300). We didn't have a coffee pit, and since I dislike instant coffee (that's what most people drink here), I had to figure out a way to make coffee. So, I bought a Chinese made, 1-litre thermos for $3.00, put coarsely-ground locally produced coffee in it, poured boiling water on it, and in 15 minutes the coffee was ready. I drink part of it for breakfast, and the rest for lunch. Since the coffee is coarsely ground, and is not disturbed much, the brew is quite clear when poured, only the last bit is like 'Fraser mud.'"

If you don't have a tea-pot, tea can be made by merely placing some tea leave in a pot, pouring boiling water over it and covering the pit with a lid or plate to allow the tea to steep.

COOKING VEGETABLES

All vegetables, which grow above the ground, should be put into boiling water, and all those, which grow underneath in cold water.

measures

TIME TABLES FOR COOKING VEGETABLES

Beans	15-25 minutes according to age
Cabbage	15-25 minutes according to size
Onions	30-40 minutes
Sweet Corn	15-20 minutes
Potatoes	20-30 minutes according to size
Pumpkin	15-25 minutes
Yam	15-20 minutes easily overcooked
Taro	20-30 minutes according to size
Spinach	15-20 minutes
Native Greens	10-15 minutes easily overcooked
Chokoes	30-35 minutes according to size
Pitpit roasted in coals	30-40 minutes according to heat
Cucumbers	15-20 minutes
Pawpaw Roasted	20-30 minutes - cook in skin
Rice, White	15-20 minutes
Rice, Brown	30-45 minutes

FLOUR

Taro, yam, tapioca, breadfruit or green cooking or eating bananas
1. Wash and peel the roots or fruit.
2. Cut into thin slices.
3. Put the slices on a wooden or bamboo rack.
4. Dry in the sun until the slices are crisp and will snap easily. This will take several days.
5. Cover or take inside at night or when it rains, to make flour pound or roll out with a stone on a piece of board. Sift. Keep in a dry place.

USES:
1. Instead of oats to make porridge.
2. Instead of wheat flour for thickening sauces and stews.
3. Instead of part of the wheat flour in bread, cakes, scones, biscuits and pastry.

FOOD STORAGE

Canned food deteriorates more rapidly in the tropics. Check the tins carefully when you buy them. If the top of the can is raised, the contents are bad. If the can is badly dented, a microscopic hole could have resulted and contents will be deteriorating. Be suspicious of rusted cans, they could be very old stock.

Don't leave any food open as/or you will be invaded by cockroaches, flies, and ants. Store everything in old-jars or ice cream containers and wipe your cupboards and containers very regularly.

measures

Part 4: Additional Information-Australian Measures

104

Part 4: Additional Information-Australian Measures

Another method is to buy some small-hole fly wire and build a safe. Stand the legs of the safe in empty cans into which you pour water and then float kerosene on top of it. No ant can swim through this.

COCKROACH DESTROYER

4 parts cocoa; 9 parts starch; 36 parts borax.
Mix together and put in saucers about the house at night.

Don't buy large quantities of flour and rice because of weevils. Small weevils can be picked or sifted out but once they begin to nest, the food will have to be destroyed. It is often a good idea to check packages in the store, as it is quite possible to buy a box of cereal or whatever well-nested with weevils.

Place bay leaves in your containers of flour and rice, as they seem to retard the development of weevils.

Butter can be kept in a small open container standing in a large open dish of cold water. Drop an absorbent cloth over the smaller container so that the ends fall into the water and keep in a draughty place. Evaporation keeps the butter from melting in the heat, but the water level needs replenishing from time to time. Use the same method for fluid milk.

Baking powder and yeast tend to deteriorate rapidly so buy in small quantities and store in tightly sealed containers.

MEAT PRESERVATION

1. Cover with a wet cloth and hang in cool shady spot. Keep cloth wet or hang in saucepan with wet cloth over top. This gives better protection from animals.
2. Meat can be kept for days by cooking and placing it in a can or jar and completely covering it with lard. The lard keeps out the air.
3. Rub salt on the meat and sprinkle lemon juice or vinegar on it.
4. Pressure cook fresh meat for the full amount of time. Every day until the meat is all used, bring it up to pressure for a few minutes to keep it from spoiling.

INNOVATIONS

tables

To make string: Scorch a banana leaf in a hot fire, and then take out the centre stem. Scorch the stem some more then pull off the strips and use as string.
To make a food grater: Cut a large Sunshine Milk tin in half and pierce holes with a large nail.
To make bowls: Use clean coconut shells.
To make a steamer: Place food in a coconut shell, cover with a leaf and place in a saucepan of water to steam. Place lid on the saucepan tightly.

TABLE OF SUBSTITUTIONS

Ingredient	Amount	Substitute
Baking powder	1 teaspoon	• 2 teaspoon vinegar plus 2 teaspoon soda • 2 teaspoon soda plus 1 teaspoon cream of tartar • juice of 1 lime plus 1 t. soda
Butter	1 cup	• 1 cup margarine • 1 cup shortening • 7/8 cup lard plus 2 teaspoon salt
Chocolate	1 square, unsweetened	3 tablespoons cocoa plus 1 tablespoon shortening or butter
Cream	1 cup	7/8 cup milk plus 3 tablespoons butter
Eggs	1 whole egg	• 2 egg yolks • 2 cup milk plus 1 teaspoon baking powder plus 1 tablespoon vinegar
Flour (for thickener)	1 tablespoon	• 2 tablespoon cornstarch • 2 teaspoons quick cooking tapioca • 2 tablespoons grated tapioca
Honey	1 cup	1 cup granulated sugar plus ¼ cup water
Lemongrass		grated lemon rind
Milk	1 cup whole milk	• 1 cup skim milk plus 2 teaspoons butter • 2 cup evaporated milk plus ½ cup water
Yeast	1 oz. compressed 1 package	1 tablespoon granulated yeast

ABBREVIATIONS
see conversion tables on page 108

t. (tsp) - Teaspoon
T. - Tablespoon
c. - Cup
F - Fahrenheit
lb - pound
pkg - package

tables

GUIDE TO HIGH ALTITUDE ADJUSTMENTS IN BAKING

Adjustment	3000 feet (900 meters) above sea level	5000 feet (1500 meters)	7000 feet (2100 meters)
Increase liquid: for each cup add	1-2 table-spoons	2-3 tablespoons	3-4 tablespoons
Reduce baking powder: for each teaspoon decrease	1/8 teaspoon	1/8–¼ teaspoon	¼ – ½ teaspoons
Reduce sugar: for each cup decrease	---------	----------	1-2 tablespoons
Increase flour: for each cup add	---------	----------	1-2 teaspoons

This is a guide. You will have to experiment, starting with smaller adjustments.

OTHER ADJUSTMENTS FOR BAKING AT HIGH ALTITUDES

Cupcakes and layer cakes: 10 - 15 increase in baking temperature may give better results.

Cookies and pastry: May need to increase flour with Canadian recipes

Rich cakes: Slight reduction in shortening sometimes necessary

Candies, jams and jellies: Will cook faster

Yeast breads: Rising' time may be reduced. Oven temperature increased by 10 or 15 F. Bake loaves at higher temperature (425 F) for first 15 minutes; then reduce temperature to that of the recipe for the remainder of the baking time if using a gas stove. Does not seem to matter with solid fuel.

tables

Conversion Chart for Fahrenheit (F) and Celcius (C)

Fahrenheit	Celcius
250	120
275	135
300	150
325	170
350	180
375	190
400	200
425	220
450	230

Conversion Chart for Other Measurements

English or US Units	Metric
1 teaspoon (t)	5 ml
1 tablespoon (T)	15 ml
1 cup (c)	240 ml
1 pound (lb)	453 gm (roughly ½ kg)
1 ounce (oz)	28 gm
1 pint	473 ml
1 inch	2.54 cm

Part 4: Additional Information-Australian Measures

Tables

My Recipes

Personal Notes: My Recipes.....

Notes

109

My Recipes

Notes

My Recipes

Personal Notes: My Recipes.....

Notes

My Recipes

Notes

My Recipes

Notes

My Recipes

Notes

114

My Recipes

Personal Notes: My Recipes.....

Notes

My Recipes

Notes

116

My Recipes

Notes

My Recipes

Notes

My Recipes

Notes

119

My Recipes

Notes

Breinigsville, PA USA
10 January 2011
252946BV00004B/5/P